William White

Sir Lyon Playfair Taken to Pieces and Disposed of: Likewise Sir Charles W. Dilke, Bart.

Being a dissection of their speeches in the House of Commons, on 19th June, 1883,

in defence of compulsory vaccination

William White

Sir Lyon Playfair Taken to Pieces and Disposed of: Likewise Sir Charles W. Dilke, Bart.
*Being a dissection of their speeches in the House of Commons, on 19th June, 1883, in defence
of compulsory vaccination*

ISBN/EAN: 9783337254162

Printed in Europe, USA, Canada, Australia, Japan

Cover: Foto ©Suzi / pixelio.de

More available books at **www.hansebooks.com**

SIR LYON PLAYFAIR

Taken to Pieces and Disposed of:

LIKEWISE

SIR CHARLES W. DILKE, Bart.

Being a Dissection of their Speeches

in the House of Commons, on 19th June, 1883,

in Defence of Compulsory Vaccination.

By WILLIAM WHITE.

London:

EDWARD W. ALLEN, 4 AVE MARIA LANE.

1884.

Glasgow:
Printed by Hay Nisbet & Co.,
38 Stockwell Street.

PREFACE.

WE heard Sir Lyon Playfair's speech in the House of Commons, and thought it a dashing and unscrupulous performance, adapted for immediate effect, which would soon pass away; but we appear to have over-estimated popular perspicacity. The speech still haunts the newspapers, and is referred to by M.P.'s in answer to their constituents as a sufficient defence of their votes. Moreover, along with Sir Charles Dilke's, it has been produced in an "authorised edition," which is scattered broadcast wherever there is any agitation against Vaccination.

We find, too, that the speech is an old one, having been delivered in the House of Commons in 1870; and Dr. Garth Wilkinson, in *Smallpox and Vaccination*, published in 1871, thus deals with the arguments we encounter again in the following pages—

" Dr. Lyon Playfair, in a clever speech, traced the
" statistics of the decline of Smallpox coincidently with
" the terrific frowns of the House of Commons, embodied
" against the monster in the various Vaccinatory Laws
" culminating in the last Act of Universal Compulsory
" Vaccination. He made out most beautifully that every

" fresh turn of the Parliamentary screw wrung the
" withers of the disease ; and that complete compulsion
" would banish it from the earth. John Bull entire had
" only to take Jane Cow in his arms, and they two would
" defy the foe. Unhappily for the beauty of his statis-
" tics, they were pitted with a few afterthoughts. In the
" first place, the diminished death-rate was so immediate
" on Act after Act of Parliament, that the effect was
" clean against him, if Vaccination were supposed to
" enter into it. The Smallpox might have been fright-
" ened by the Laws, but could not have been hurt. In
" the second place, the Acts were at first coincident
" with outbursts of Smallpox, after which, decline of the
" disease is the way of Nature : proving that the coin-
" cidence is by a Natural Law. In the third place,
" which seams the face of the Doctor's speech from
" vertex to chin, and puts out its eyes—after the Law
" of General Compulsory Vaccination has had time to
" work, and has worked, a worse outbreak of Smallpox
" than before occurs ; and has to be accounted for by
" the statistician on some grounds quite different from
" the power of Parliament through Vaccinatory Laws
" over Smallpox."

Dr. W. J. Collins provided an admirable and adequate
reply to the speech of 19th June, in a pamphlet entitled
Sir Lyon Playfair's Logic, to which any supplement
would seem superfluous. Some, however, who read
Dr. Collins say they would like to peruse Sir Lyon
Playfair afresh before consenting to surrender ; whilst
others consider that Sir Lyon should be categorically
answered.

Taking these circumstances and demands into consideration, it appeared to us that perhaps the longest way would prove the shortest, and that we could not do better than reprint the authorised reports of Sir Lyon Playfair and Sir Charles Dilke's speeches in full, dividing them into convenient sections, and adjoining to each what we consider a sufficient reply. Than this, it will be admitted, nothing could be fairer. We let each adversary state his case without the alteration of a word, subjoining our answer, and leaving the reader to decide between us. We have no reason to shrink from the statistics and arguments of Sir Lyon Playfair ; we merely claim the justice of being heard in reply. In the end it will be admitted that we have justified our title—that we have taken the speech of Sir Lyon Playfair to pieces and disposed of it, so that when next he addresses the House of Commons upon Vaccination he will have to provide himself with something different.

A heavy Nonconformist vote contributed to swell the majority against Mr. Taylor's motion ; affording an illustration of the inanimate fashion in which many hold what they are pleased to call their "principles." They are all right as long as their principles run in the traditional groove, but when they are called to apply them in unaccustomed circumstances, they utterly break down, and go over to the multitude. It would not require a dialectician of any extraordinary skill to turn

upon these gentlemen this vote for established and endowed Vaccination, and ask them with what face they
can demand the disestablishment and disendowment of
a Church, whose claims are infinitely superior to that of
a superstitious practice they hold it right to pay for out
of public moneys, and force upon unbelievers with fine
and imprisonment.

Among these inconsistent professors was Mr. Henry
Richard, leader of Dissenters in the House of Commons,
and secretary of the Peace Society; and one who was
moved by the spectacle of his inconsistency, wrote to
him saying, that he at least ought to have shown sympathy with a people persecuted for conscience sake—

" The principle of all aggressive war and all persecu-
" tion is the determination to force compliance against
" conviction.   I who know that Vaccination is useless
" against Smallpox, and not only useless but dangerous
" in itself, am to be fined and imprisoned because I
" refuse to surrender my intelligence to the ignorance
" and superstition of a majority—inclusive of Henry
" Richard! If it is conceded that you are right in this
" enforcement of Vaccination, then I ask, What is there
" wanting, save considerations of expediency, to justify
" any persecution or any war that a majority may
" favour?

" Supposing Vaccination to be as beneficial as asserted,
" I maintain you can have no right to force it upon me.
" But descending from this high ground to the question
" of the usefulness of the practice, I entreat you to spare

" a little time to the objections advanced by Mr. P. A.
" Taylor and others. You, as a leader of minorities,
" know the fabulous defences that are thrown around
" every popular craze, and how their plausibility is fre-
" quently the measure of their falsehood. Consider
" whether this may not likewise be the case with Vacci-
" nation. You have a long and honourable record, and
" I make bold to say the time will come when it will be
" cited as a curious instance of inconsistency that Henry
" Richard, the advocate of freedom and peace at home
" and abroad, gave his vote in favour of the persecution
" of Anti-Vaccinators."

To this remonstrance Mr. Richard replied—

" It is one of the painful incidents of public life that
" one is sometimes obliged to give a vote against the
" views of esteemed friends. I can only say that I gave
" that vote conscientiously, after having carefully read
" some of my friend Mr. Peter Taylor's pamphlets, and
" listened with the utmost attention and respect to his
" speech. There is no man in the House whose char-
" acter I more honour, and it was with great regret and
" considerable hesitation I voted against him. I hope
" I am still open to conviction if adequate evidence can
" be produced; but as at present advised, I am obliged
" to believe that Vaccination is a protection against
" Smallpox."

In a sense this reply was encouraging, for its feebleness and inconsequence prove how slight was the conviction which sustained some of those who voted against
Mr. Taylor. Mr. Richard's correspondent rejoined—

" ' As at present advised,' you say, ' I am obliged to
" ' believe that Vaccination is a protection against Small-
" ' pox.'

" I cannot control your advisers, but because you
" derive from them faith in Vaccination, what reason is
" that for your trying to force your derivative faith on
" those who have none?—driving citizens, otherwise
" loyal, into the preaching and practice of resistance to
" law. The Churchman is advised that his Church is a
" protection from the world, the flesh, and the devil ; but
" what is your answer when he insists on your support
" for his Church? and what would be your answer if he
" tried to force you to observe its rites? To vote for
" Compulsory Vaccination is to surrender the cardinal
" principle of civil and religious liberty, and to establish
" a precedent for the exercise of any form of tyranny
" (for what despotism does not vindicate itself as for the
" public good?) precisely as you do when, because you
" are advised Vaccination is a protection from Smallpox,
" you insist on inflicting the horrible thing upon me.
" Try, I entreat you, to put yourself in my place in this
" matter, and then say how you would like to be scourged
" with a compulsory law."

Cases like this of Mr. Richard prove how thin is the
soil in which English liberty is rooted, and how ready it
is to wither away. In a letter Mr. Herbert Spencer
observes—

" I wish I had known some time since that Vaccina-
" tion Persecution had in any case been carried so far as
" you describe, as I should have made use of the fact.

" It would have served farther to enforce the parallel
" between this Medical Popery which men think so
" defensible and the Religious Popery which they think
" so indefensible."

One observation remains, which I urge every reader
to bear firmly in mind. It is the convenient habit of
Vaccinators to speak of Vaccination as uniform, and as
if the Virus of the rite were as definite as a drop of
water, a pinch of salt, or a grain of gold. Nothing can
be more erroneous. The Virus described as Vaccine is
not one but various, not uniform but multiform, not
certain but uncertain with an uncertainty which in
transit from body to body can neither be predicated nor
ascertained. The Vaccinator's art is of all arts the most
empirical. The matter on his lancet he cannot define,
and the issue from the matter he cannot foretell.

The Virus is not one but various. The Local Government Board claim to vaccinate with stocks derived
from Jenner, but Jenner was responsible for at least
three diverse stocks. His original prescription was
Horsegrease Cowpox. He then, to circumvent compe-
titors, went in for Cowpox, which he had proved to be
no defence against Smallpox. Lastly he set aside the
cow altogether, and used and diffused Horsegrease, or
Horsepox, which he described as " the true and genuine
life-preserving fluid." To these Jennerian stocks have
been added Smallpox Cowpox obtained from inocu-
lating cows with Smallpox. Mr. Lowe, speaking for

the Vaccine Establishment in the House of Commons in 1861, said—

" There is a theory started that the efficacy of Vacci- " nation is wearing out; but the valuable discovery of " Mr. Ceely has set any apprehension on that score at " rest for ever. Mr. Ceely has proved that Smallpox, " when taken from the human body and introduced to " that of the cow, produces Cowpox. It is thus evident " that we have the means of obtaining Cowpox of the " requisite strength to any extent. The beautiful dis- " covery has also been made that the security of Vac- " cination may be almost indefinitely increased by " multiplying the number of punctures."

Thus we have virus derived from Horsegrease Cow-pox, from Cowpox, from Horsepox, and from Smallpox Cowpox commingled with the constitutional character-istics of the ranks of Vaccinifers through which the diverse poxes have passed ; and which is which, and how modified for better or for worse in the course of travel none know or can know. Latterly, to allay pub-lic alarm concerning the invaccination of Syphilis, a Cowpox Factory has been opened in Lamb's Conduit Street, where virus of mysterious origin is propagated on the abdomens of heifers. And these different poxes, indefinitely and inscrutably varied, are inoculated on universal infancy, and the inoculation of all alike passes for Vaccination ; and all alike are held to work the miracle of salvation from Smallpox—or if not salvation, then of mitigation !

And the law has been adroitly accommodated to this almost incredible imposture. As Dr. Garth Wilkinson points out—

" The people at large, and probably a large part of
" the medical profession, are not aware of the sources
" from which vaccine lymph is derived. What is more
" strange, the Vaccination Acts, under the compulsion
" of which our homes lie, *give no definition of what that*
" *Vaccination is* which we are compelled to undergo.
" The practical solution appears to be, *that whatever a*
" *legally qualified practitioner affirms to be Vaccination,* IS
" *Vaccination.* In this fundamental matter, Vaccination
" Law differs from almost all other law, in that all
" statutes, either commanding something, or prohibit-
" ing something, or limiting something, state what that
" something is. Vaccination Law makes no declaration
" of the kind."

It is precisely so: the Law does not define Vaccination, and whatever a legally qualified practitioner calls
Vaccination *is* Vaccination.

There was an Act passed in 1840, and re-enacted in
1867, prohibiting inoculation with Smallpox, and the use
of Smallpox Cowpox is without doubt an infraction of the
terms of that Act. Indeed, the Irish Local Government
Board in 1879 forbade the generation of such Variolous
Cowpox on the ground that " it would communicate
Smallpox and render the operator liable to prosecution."
Yet what was thus proscribed by authority in Ireland
has been freely practised in England, and the resulting

Smallpox Cowpox has been included in the national stock and passed into currency beyond identification !

On the other hand, the German Hufeland by the application of Tartarated Antimony, otherwise Tartar Emetic, to the skin produced vesicles similar in character to those of Cowpox, and, as he truly maintained, equally prophylactic. The discovery was shelved, we believe, for no other reason than its shameless simplicity, which was supposed to discredit the Jennerian mystery.

There is nothing to hinder any qualified practitioner reviving Hufeland's practice. It would be Vaccination if he chose to call it Vaccination. We mention these extremes, Smallpox Cowpox and Tartar Emetic, to illustrate the extraordinary character of the law.

Dr. Balthazar Foster recently observed at a meeting of the British Medical Association, that "it was incom- "prehensible how the virtue of Vaccination could be " regarded as an open question by any scientifically " educated mind ;" but he forgot to state which variety of Vaccination. The several varieties cannot all be virtuous, or equally virtuous. Dr. Foster is surely aware that Science and Vaccination have never come to a reckoning. There is scarcely an affirmation made by any authority relative to Vaccination that is not contradicted by some other authority equally good ; and such being the case, how shall we affiliate Vaccination with Science ? Science has been defined as verified and reasoned knowledge ; and, if the definition be correct, what claim has the medley of practice and fancy, designated Vaccination, to do with Science? Dr. Foster and his associates had better rest satisfied with Vaccination as a Mystery, publicly endowed and privately lucrative. As a Mystery it exists, but whenever the methods of Science are applied to it, there will be an exposure and an explosion—and alas ! disestablishment and disendowment. Wherefore, Dr. Foster and his associates will show themselves wise in their generation if they talk as little as possible about Science and Vaccination. The juxtaposition is dangerous, and a shock may precipitate disaster.

CONTENTS.

SIR LYON PLAYFAIR'S SPEECH.

19th June, 1883.

I.—PRELIMINARY.

UNEXPECTEDLY an opportunity was secured for the discussion of Vaccination in the House of Commons on 19th June, 1883, when Mr. P. A. Taylor moved—

"That in the opinion of this House it is inexpedient " and unjust to enforce Vaccination under penalties upon " those who regard it as unadvisable and dangerous."

On Tuesday evenings it is difficult to form a House of forty members, and a "count-out" is a frequent incident. On this occasion a count-out was attempted but frustrated, and Mr. Taylor was enabled to proceed with his argument. His speech possessed every requisite for the conversion of the unconverted ; but it cannot be too widely known that the great majority of the members who subsequently voted against him were conspicuous by absence. Their recorded judgment was that of those who had heard but one side of the question. They were ignorant and prejudiced to start with, and had their ignorance confirmed and their prejudice stimulated by so much as they were pleased to listen to. Let not this

I

condition of the debate be lost sight of, nor its influence on the conclusion. Mr. Hopwood seconded the motion in an admirable address, lucid and cogent. Meanwhile, it having become obvious that a division was inevitable, there was a marked increase in attendance, for a snap vote adverse to Vaccination would have been accounted an insufferable mishap. Sir Joseph Pease then rose, and moved as an amendment—

"That a Select Committee of the House be appointed
"for the purpose of ascertaining whether a limitation of
"the accumulation of penalties for non-vaccination can
"be effected without endangering the practical efficiency
"of the Vaccination Acts."

In the end this amendment was withdrawn, Sir Charles Dilke expressing the concurrence of the Government in the expediency of limiting penalties for non-vaccination, but questioning the likelihood of obtaining the assent of Parliament to the concession—a notable indication of the mind and temper of the House of Commons as at present constituted. Sir Lyon Playfair rose to reply, and ultimately moved—

"That in the opinion of this House the practice of
"Vaccination has greatly lessened the mortality from
"Smallpox, and that laws relating to it, with such modi-
"fications as experience may suggest, are necessary for
"the prevention and mitigation of this fatal and mutila-
"tive disease."

Always curious and eager to hear what can be urged in justification of a practice which is a survival from the pre-scientific age, we followed Sir Lyon Playfair atten-tively, but anything more hopelessly commonplace than his discourse it would be difficult to imagine. The

stalest fallacies of the vaccinators were recited as if they
had never been answered. The freshness consisted in
the business-like assurance and plausibility, after the
Scots manner, with which the speech was delivered.
Not a single novel point was made. Still, to those who
knew no better, it was a capital speech, and was received
with acclamation, especially from the Conservative side.
We all love to have our prejudices flattered, and never
more than when we suspect them to be questionable.
Sir Charles Dilke congratulated Sir Lyon on his brilliant
vindication of the virtues of Vaccination, and proceeded
to enforce them with a variety of details from the reper-
tory of Dr. Buchanan—he who recently informed the
public that the lives of 12,000 London infants were
saved annually by Vaccination! The House was in the
humour for marvels. Sir Trevor Lawrence repeated the
story of Escott's coat and the Rotherhithe epidemic,
and it was plain that if anyone had produced a dozen
similar fables from his fancy, they would have had an
uproarious welcome. The hour was late, and the House
impatient of contradiction when Mr. Taylor replied, and
it was useless to prolong discussion. When the division
took place, the numbers were—

For Sir Lyon Playfair's amendment,...... 286
Against,... 16
                                                        ———
        Majority,.......................... 270

The minority of 16—or, including the tellers, 18—is
entitled to honourable record. They were as follows—

ARTHUR ARNOLD, Salford.
JOHN BARRAN, Leeds.
R. P. BLENNERHASSETT, Co. Kerry.

JACOB BRIGHT, Manchester.
THOMAS BURT, Morpeth.
SIR THOMAS CHAMBERS, Marylebone.
ARTHUR COHEN, Southwark.
JOSEPH COWEN, Newcastle.
WILLIAM Y. CRAIG, North Staffordshire.
ROBERT FERGUSON, Carlisle.
JOHN R. HOLLOND, Brighton.
C. H. HOPWOOD, Stockport.
JAMES HOWARD, Bedfordshire.
HENRY LABOUCHERE, Northampton.
SIR WILFRID LAWSON, Carlisle.
THOMAS ROE, Derby.
J. E. THOROLD ROGERS, Southwark.
P. A. TAYLOR, Leicester.

There are not a few names absent from the list which ought to have been present; and, worse still, some of them on the opposite list; but we make allowance. Every commander knows that there are soldiers brave enough for ordinary duty, who are morally unfit for any arduous enterprise. And so it is in politics. The mass of M.P.'s follow their leaders loyally, but when it comes to independent action, why then they bolt, as several of them did on the night of 19th June. A valuable result of the division is the discovery of the trustworthy, and of those who stand in need of restoratives, which, doubtless, their constituents will liberally administer. Until this division, it could not be said that the question of Compulsory Vaccination had come within the range of practical politics. Now it has acquired that distinction, and there it will abide until disposed of. Anti-Vaccinists are powerful in many constituencies, and are rapidly gaining ground in others, and henceforth Vaccination will be a test question; and unless candidates give a distinct pledge that they will vote for the repeal of compulsion, the ballot will exhibit the consequences.

The reception of the verdict of the House of Commons by the leading newspapers could only be described as delirious. We were told that any question as to the efficacy of Vaccination was settled, and that the fanatics led by Mr. Taylor had received their quietus. If we had no memories we might be discouraged, but having seen the like ordeal of abuse and extinction so frequently survived, and the survivors invigorated by the process, it cost little to maintain equanimity. Fifty years ago the fallacy that it was possible by protective duties levied on imports to promote the national wealth and welfare was as completely exploded by science as at this day is the fallacy that it is possible by Vaccination to avert Small-pox and promote health. Yet the annual motions of Mr. Villiers for the repeal of the Corn Laws were rejected by crushing majorities in the House of Commons; and with each defeat it was predicted that he and his associated fanatics had received their quietus. Even so advanced a Whig as Sydney Smith stigmatised the projected repeal as "nonsensical." Lord Melbourne, the Whig Premier, declared, with the exultant approval of both sides of the House, that—

"During my long life it has been my lot to hear many mad things proposed; but the maddest of all the mad things to which I have ever had to listen, is a proposal to abolish the Corn Laws."

When a deputation of Free-Traders from Manchester waited upon Sir James Graham in 1840, he told them—

"If the Corn Laws were repealed, great disasters would fall upon the country. The land would go out of cultivation. Church and State could not be upheld. In short all our institutions would be reduced to their primitive elements, and the people you are now exciting would pull down our houses about our ears."

Yet within a few years of these utterances, the Corn
Laws were swept away, and the fanatics were recognised
as national benefactors. The like will happen when
science (now latent to many) makes an end of the protection supposed to be conferred by Vaccination. Such
transformations are under continual repetition in human
nature. In a propitious hour, the adversaries of truth,
often insensibly to themselves, are carried over to the
side they have hitherto regarded with hatred and terror.
Bearing such phenomena in mind, why should we suffer
dismay because the House of Commons voted according
to prejudice on 19th June, after avoiding the indictment
of Mr. Taylor? How, indeed, granting the circumstances, could the House have voted otherwise? None
can say Mr. Taylor's contention was rejected, for by the
majority it was unheard.

Whatever our opinion of the intrinsic merits of Sir
Lyon Playfair's speech, it would be folly to minimise its
importance. It is the official vindication of Vaccination,
and as such was accepted by the House of Commons.
One of his auditors observed, "If nothing better can be
said by vaccinators for their art, then [in Cromwell's
phrase] hath the Lord delivered them into our hands."
It may be so, but it is for us to communicate our conviction to others; and as one way of doing so we have
resolved to reply to Sir Lyon Playfair's speech seriatim;
first citing each statement in full from the authorised
report, and then adjoining what we think every candid
reader will allow to be an answer more or less conclusive.
We Anti-Vaccinists are accustomed to victory wherever
we obtain a hearing.

II.—The Prohibition of Vaccination.

Sir Lyon Playfair in moving his amendment started with saying—

" The resolution of my Hon. Friend, the Member for
" Leicester, must be read between the lines as a distinct
" attack on Vaccination, root and branch.   In the mind
" of my Hon. Friend, Vaccination itself is an evil thing,
" and ought to be extirpated.   If he so believe, his
" resolution ought to express his belief, and he should
" bring in a Prohibitory Act, as was done in the case of
" Inoculation with Smallpox in 1840."

The observation is significant.   Supposing Vaccination to be an evil thing, it is said that Mr. Taylor should introduce a bill for the punishment of those who are convinced it is their only defence against Smallpox ! Inasmuch as Mr. Taylor contends " that it is inexpedient and unjust to enforce Vaccination upon those who regard it as unadvisable and dangerous," with what grace could he propose to commit an aggression on those who are persuaded it is advisable and harmless ?   Mr. Taylor has neither part nor lot with those who endeavour to enforce practices accounted good, and to prohibit practices accounted bad, by Act of Parliament.   There are no limits to the projects for the compulsory welfare of the people ; and it would not surprise us if a group of philanthropic and enterprising M.P.'s brought in a bill for the monthly medical inspection of everybody, with penalties for whoever failed to report himself and family to the district inspector, or refused to submit to the regimen or swallow the medicine prescribed.   How easy it would be to recommend such legislation with evidence and arguments of the most conclusive character! It is not in this direction, however, that we are prepared to walk. So many, so great, and so sweet are the fruits of freedom, that we account its accidents and drawbacks as trivialities for which the most beneficent and omnipotent of despotisms would be a poor exchange. In this connection we recall the noble words of Cobbett addressed to Wilberforce in 1803—

> "I like not this never-ending recurrence to Acts of Parliament. Something must be left, and something *ought* to be left, to the sense and reason and morality and religion of the people. There are a set of *well-meaning men* in this country, who would pass laws for the regulating and restraining of every feeling of the human breast, and every motion of the human frame: they would bind us down, hair by hair, as the Lilliputians did Gulliver, till anon, when we awoke from our sleep, we should wonder by whom we had been enslaved. But I trust, Sir, that Parliament is not, and never will be, so far under the influence of these minute and meddling politicians as to be induced to pass laws for taking out of a man's hands the management of his household, the choice of his physician, and the care of the health of his children; for, under this sort of domiciliary thraldom, to talk of the liberty of the country would be the most cruel mockery wherewith an humble and subjected people were ever insulted."

We are of Bishop Lightfoot's opinion, "It is better that men should do wrong believing it to be right, than that they should be forced to do right believing it to be wrong." There is no education like experience; for the pains and penalties attached to error give lessons with a precision and persistence from which there is no evasion. If Vaccination be a sure defence against Smallpox, suffering and terror may be trusted to ensure its observance; and hence we may reasonably assume that those who make gain by the practice are clamorous for its continued enforcement because they feel it could not maintain itself by the evidence of its efficiency.

III.—Vaccinia itself a Disease.

" Mr. Taylor and the Society with which he acts
" attack Vaccination on two grounds. The first is, that
" it is positively injurious, as a means of introducing dis-
" ease into the bodies of the vaccinated ; and the second
" is, that it has no protective power against Smallpox,
" which it is supposed to prevent or mitigate.

" The assertion that Vaccination produces disease was
" carefully examined by a Committee of the House of
" Commons in 1871, of which Committee Mr. Taylor was
" an active member, and he will bear me out when I say
" that we carefully heard the evidence of the Anti-Vacci-
" nators and formed a unanimous conclusion expressed
" in the words of the report, ' That there need be no
" ' apprehension that Vaccination will injure health or
" ' communicate any disease.' It is true that Mr. Taylor
" moved the omission of these words, but what were those
" which he proposed to substitute ? They were these—
" ' That some few cases of disease have been communi-
" ' cated by Vaccination, but the danger is so infinitesi-
" ' mal in respect to proportion that the Committee do
" ' not hesitate to express their conviction of the practi-
" ' cally safe character of the operation.' I think, then,
" as the Hon. Member for Leicester after hearing the
" evidence characterised the danger ' as infinitesimal in
" ' respect of proportion,' I need not trouble the House
" with any further remarks on this branch of the subject."

Mr. Taylor's position at this day is the best commentary upon his opinion in 1871; and it is to his honour
that he has not only made no secret of the change in
his judgment, but that he has set himself to effect a
corresponding change in the judgment of his fellow-
legislators.

The loose and unscientific habit of Sir Lyon Playfair's
mind is apparent in his adoption of the opinion " that

there need be no apprehension that Vaccination will injure health or communicate any disease." Why, it is the purpose of Vaccination to communicate disease, and to the extent of the disease to injure health! Mr. Pepper on a recent occasion defined Vaccination as the production of "an acute specific disease." Mr. John Simon replying to the question, "Whether properly performed Vaccination is an absolutely inoffensive proceeding?" answers, "Not at all; nor does it pretend to be so." And Dr. Ballard, Medical Officer to the Local Government Board, in his treatise, *Vaccination: its Value and Alleged Dangers*, says—

"Vaccination is not a thing to be trifled with, or to be made light of; it is not to be undertaken thoughtlessly or without due consideration of the condition of the patient, his mode of life, and the circumstances of season and of place. Surgeon and patient should both carry in their minds the regulating thought that the one is engaged in communicating, the other in receiving into his system a *real* disease—as truly a disease as Smallpox or Measles; a disease which, mild and gentle as its progress may usually be, yet, nevertheless, now and then, like every other exanthematous malady, asserts its character by an unusual exhibition of virulence."

If, therefore, it were possible to communicate Vaccinia as Vaccinia and nothing else, we should still protest against it as a wilful generation of disease, as an aggression on health, and as a reduction of that vigour or vitality which is not only the best defence against Smallpox, but against every other ailment.

IV.—THE INVACCINATION OF SYPHILIS.

"The allegation that Vaccination has been known to
" produce Syphilis was practically proved in a few cases
" in which vaccine lymph had been taken from children
" suffering from congenital Syphilis. The possibility of
" such infection is a terrible fact, but, fortunately, one of

" the extremest rarity. We had it in evidence that
" among 151,316 revaccinations of soldiers, not one such
" case had ever been observed, although among them
" Syphilis is far from rare. Since 1852, about 17 million
" infants have been vaccinated in England and Wales,
" and among these, if there were any large truth in the
" allegations, not tens but hundreds of cases must have
" been observed; and yet it is extremely doubtful whether
" half-a-dozen central cases of propagation have been
" reasonably suspected."

Here we have a daring draft on ignorance and credulity. It is said, " If there were any large truth in the
allegation that Vaccination has been known to produce
Syphilis, not tens but hundreds of cases must have been
observed." Now, there is this peculiarity about Syphilis
—it often takes time to manifest itself, so that between
invaccination and discovery, the origin of the malady is
questioned or denied. Mr. R. Brudenell Carter, whose
competence will not be disputed, thus describes the
case—

"I think that Syphilitic contamination by Vaccine Lymph is by no means
an unusual occurrence, and that it is very generally overlooked because
people do not know either when or where to look for it. I think that a large
proportion of the cases of apparently inherited Syphilis are in reality Vac-
cinal; and that the Syphilis in these cases does not show itself until the age
of from eight to ten years, by which time the relation between cause and
effect is apt to be lost sight of."

Dr. Ballard, in 1868, adduced a variety of evidence
which led to these decisive conclusions—

"1.—There are *numerous cases on record* to prove that the Vaccine
Virus and the Syphilitic Virus may be introduced at the same spot by the
same puncture of the vaccinating lancet.

"2.—From several instances on record, there can remain no reasonable
doubt that the Vaccine Virus and Syphilitic Virus may both be drawn at
the same time, upon the same instrument, from one and the same Vesicle.

"3.—The Vesicle which is thus capable of furnishing both Vaccine and
Syphilitic Virus may present, prior to being opened, all the normal and
fully-developed characters of a true Jennerian Vesicle, as ordinarily met
with."

The returns of the Registrar-General, moreover, show that deaths from Syphilis have been steadily increasing in England and Wales. In 1838-42 they were 10.6 per million; in 1860-64 they had risen to 63.6 per million; and in 1875-79 they had gone up to 85.7 per million, being in excess of the death-rate of Smallpox itself, which in 1876-80 stood at 78.4 per million. There is little reason to doubt that this startling increase of Syphilitic Mortality is largely due to the invaccination of the malady. At the same time, be it remembered, the number of deaths thus registered but faintly indicates the misery and the ruined lives throughout the land, which are unentered in the column of Syphilitic Mortality.

Time was when the possibility of the invaccination of Syphilis was altogether denied by vaccinators, spite of much evidence to the contrary; but facts adduced by Mr. Jonathan Hutchinson and others at last prevailed; and Sir Thomas Watson, breaking through the etiquette of his profession, openly confessed to the "ghastly risk" in *The Nineteenth Century*, saying—

"I can readily sympathise with, and even applaud, a father who, with the presumed dread and misgiving in his mind, is willing to submit to multiplied judicial penalties rather than expose his child to the risk of an infection so ghastly."

Much has been learnt since the Committee sat in 1871, and it is too late in the day to talk of the invaccination of Syphilis being "a possibility of the extremest rarity." The condemnation of Vaccination from arm-to-arm, and the resort to calves for virus, alike on the Continent and the United States, attest the reality and frequency of a danger which it is idle to gainsay. To appease the alarm excited in this country, the Government opened an establishment in Lamb's Conduit Street for Bovine Vaccination; but, with characteristic perversity, set over it Dr. Cory, who was without faith in the enterprise—convinced, doubtless, like Jenner himself, that Cowpox *per se* is of no avail against Smallpox. To prove the superfluity of his appointed vocation, Dr. Cory began to experiment upon himself with vaccine virus taken from syphilitic subjects, and speedily proved in his own person that the outcry against such virus had full and frightful warrant. For Sir Lyon Playfair to assert that the invaccination of Syphilis is uncommon, is equivalent to saying that infantile Syphilis is uncommon; that the disease is recognisable in early infancy; and that syphilitic infants do not serve as vaccinifers—all which is notoriously untrue. Mr. John Simon, who used to deny the possibility of invaccinated Syphilis, observes—

"When a child is born with the heritage of Syphilis (a very frequent incident, if its parents have been suffering from that infection), *the characteristic symptoms do not appear until some weeks after birth;* and then the scandal discloses itself "—

Which is precisely what is maintained; and before disclosure the child is vaccinated, and serving as a vaccinifer, the latent disease is inoculated and diffused.

" We had it in evidence," says Sir Lyon Playfair, "that among 151,316 revaccinations of soldiers, not one case of invaccinated Syphilis had ever been observed, although Syphilis is far from rare among them." But if cases of invaccinated Syphilis had occurred, what reason is there to suppose they would either have been recognised or reported?—especially as " Syphilis is far from rare among soldiers." We have an example which vividly illustrates, first, the facility with which Syphilis may be invaccinated, and second, the insuperable difficulty there is in obtaining recognition of the fact. On 30th December, 1880,

the young soldiers of the garrison of Algiers were vaccinated. The virus used was taken from a couple of
infants, two months old, apparently in perfect health
Those vaccinated from one of the children exhibited
nothing special, but 58 vaccinated from the other, a
Spanish infant, developed in a few weeks the character-
istics of an infection which could not be mistaken—all
were attacked with Syphilis! The disaster excited
much attention. The names and regimental numbers of
the unfortunate men, who were obliged to leave the
service, were published in Algerian and French journals,
but whilst the facts were not disputed, they were not
admitted by the authorities. Questions addressed to
the Minister of War in the Chamber of Deputies were
evaded on one pretext or other; and the same course of
prevarication was resorted to in the House of Commons
when Mr. Hopwood appealed to Mr. Dodson, as President of the Local Government Board, for details and
confirmation of the disaster. About the facts, there
never was any question. They were well known to the
French medical staff, and to the medical department of
our own Local Government Board; but the official confession was not to be had on any terms. The game is
perfectly understood. We know that they know, and
they know that we know, and they know that we know
that they know. Perhaps it is as unreasonable to expect
truth under the circumstances as it is to expect the same
from respondents in the Divorce Court. The incident,
however, disposes of Sir Lyon Playfair's contention, that
because the invaccination of Syphilis is not reported by
vaccinators, it is therefore uncommon or unknown.

V.—The Invaccination and Excitation of other Diseases.

" But though this offensive disease, Syphilis, is admit-
" tedly only possible by the grossest neglect, certain skin
" diseases such as Erysipelas and Eczema, are alleged to
" be consequences of Vaccination, Admittedly, they
" may follow the irritation of Vaccination, just as they
" follow the irritation of teething, or as Erysipelas fre-
" quently appears after a surgical operation. Generally
" they are instances of *post hoc*, but in a few cases, as at
" Norwich, they are *propter hoc*. Very rarely have they
" been fatal. That they have been so in very rare
" instances does not constitute an argument against
" Vaccination. Who would forbid the use of anæsthe-
" tics in surgical operations because patients have died
" from their use? Who would stop the use of narcotics
" because to some persons they produce the sleep of
" death? Who would prevent men drinking water be-
" cause sometimes polluted water produces typhoid
" fever?

" Anti-Vaccinators attach no importance to the discov-
" eries of modern science, which clearly point to the fact
" that each disease is specific in its character, and that as
" little could you produce Bronchitis, Scrofula, or Con-
" sumption from *Vaccine Virus* as you could produce a rose
" from a cauliflower, or a mastiff from a guinea pig. That
" other diseases may produce a greater number of deaths
" when devastating Smallpox is subdued is as certain as
" the mortality of man, for if he does not die of one
" thing he will die of another. But an expensive Return
" was made to the House in 1877, giving the deaths of
" fifteen diseases before and after Vaccination. This
" Return shows that some diseases had an increased and
" some a lessened mortality; but for their purpose they
" are ludicrously perplexing. Thus, the main increase
" was in Bronchitis, which has about the same relation

" to Vaccination as the Goodwin Sands have to Ten-
" terden Steeple. Erysipelas, Scrofula, and Convulsions,
" which are the pet outcomes of Vaccination, had actu-
" ally decreased upon the whole population. Syphilis,
" indeed, had marvellously increased, but the Registrar-
" General has since told us that the classification was
" different in the first and second period, and could not
" be compared. While, therefore, fully admitting that
" man is mortal, and that he must die of something, I
" believe, both in logic and in fact, that the conclusions
" drawn from this 1877 Return are just as worthy as if
" I asked the House to accept as a conclusion that the
" few deaths of Smallpox in Ireland in 1882 were the
" causes of the increased number of Fenian assassinations
" in that year."

Expert and audacious is Sir Lyon Playfair at *petitio
principii.* The invaccination of Syphilis, he says, "is
admittedly only possible by the grossest neglect." Admitted by whom ? The contrary is the fact. All
authorities allow that by no circumspection can the
invaccination of Syphilis be avoided when humanised
virus is employed, inasmuch as the characteristic symptoms are not manifest until the mischief is done. When
the matter was under discussion in the House of Commons in 1866, Mr. Henley, the sagacious, observed—

"Undoubtedly it is an abomination to take vaccine from a diseased
child, but how is a public vaccinator to know that any child is diseased ?
If he inquires too particularly, he will run the risk of a slapped face from
the mother for his trouble."

Sir Lyon Playfair's treatment of Erysipelas is grossly
misleading, whether from ignorance or design. Erysipelas
is represented as an accident of Vaccination when it is
of its essence. Jenner, in condemning the use of Cowpox
for Vaccination, gave as his reason that "no Erysipelas

attends it"—Cowpox from Horsegrease or Horsepox being his prescription, and warranted effective by the induction of Erysipelas. So notoriously indeed is Erysipelas the result of Vaccination that it is described as its "bane" by traders in varieties of animal virus, which they guarantee not to produce the eruption. Dr. Martin of Boston, one of these traders, favoured of Dr. W. B. Carpenter, speaks of Erysipelas as "that miserable complication, the pest of vaccinators." As Dr. W. J. Collins has pointed out—

"The areola which usually surrounds Vaccine Vesicles on the eighth to the fourteenth or fifteenth day *is* Erysipelas, different from our usual conception of the latter, not in kind, but only in degree. . . . We need not be surprised, therefore, that the erysipelatous blush or areola which normally accompanies true Cowpox Vesicles, should in some cases extend indefinitely and even extensively, and occasionally lead to a fatal issue."

Erysipelas then is implied in Vaccination, and how far it may extend is dependent on the constitution, circumstances and treatment of the child vaccinated. Whether if the child should die, the death will be attributed to Vaccination, or to Erysipelas induced by Vaccination, or to Erysipelas, or to Diarrhœa induced by the Vaccination and Erysipelas, lies entirely within the discretion of the medical practitioner. Most likely he will consider it his duty to save Vaccination from reproach, and from the scandalous tongues of "those devilish Anti-Vaccinators," and will assign a cause of death as remote as possible from the first cause. In the words of Mr. May of Birmingham, who has stated the dilemma concisely and frankly—

"In certificates given by us voluntarily, and to which the public have access, it is scarcely to be expected that a medical man will give opinions which may tell against or reflect upon himself in any way, or which are likely to cause annoyance or injury to the survivors. In such cases he will likely tell the truth, but not the whole truth, *and assign some pro-*

minent symptom of the disease as the cause of death.   As instances of cases
which may tell against the medical man himself, I will mention Erysipelas
from Vaccination, and puerperal fever.   A death from the first cause
occurred not long ago in my practice, and although I had not vaccinated
the child, *yet in my desire to preserve Vaccination from reproach*, I omitted
all mention of it from my certificate of death."

Distinguishing then Erysipelas as inseparable from
Jennerian Vaccination, we come to the question whether
other diseases may like Syphilis be invaccinated ; and,
in the absence of certain information, we do not care to
discuss the point.   But setting the problem of the
limits of invaccination aside, it is firmly asserted—

1st. That Vaccination may excite latent disease ;

2nd. That it may aggravate active disease ; and

3rd. That in so far as it weakens the constitution, it
predisposes to attacks of other diseases.

Thus stated, it is seen at once how little there is in
the bouncing assumption that—

" Anti-Vaccinators attach no importance to the dis-
" coveries of modern science, which clearly point to the
" fact that each disease is specific in its character, and
" that as little could you produce Bronchitis, Scrofula, or
" Consumption from *Vaccine Virus* as you could produce
" a rose from a cauliflower, or a mastiff from a guinea
" pig."

Whoever said that Bronchitis, Scrofula, or Consumption, any more than Syphilis itself, could be generated
from Vaccine Virus *per se?*   What diseases may, in
common with Syphilis, be invaccinated, remains to be
determined ; and until determined, he is wisest who says
least.   Disease, however, kindles disease ; and many a
child might outgrow congenital Scrofula or Consumption
if the latent disorder were not roused by Vaccination.
Indeed, what is more frequent than when strumous

affections are ascribed to Vaccination to meet with the excuse, " Vaccination is not to blame : the disorder was in the sufferer's system ; Vaccination merely brought it out "—forgetting how much in all of us never comes to the surface as disease, but is overcome and cast out by natural vigour in the ordinary processes of life.

With reference to Bronchitis, which it is smartly said "has about the same relation to Vaccination as the Goodwin Sands to Tenterden Steeple," the answer is, that the debility produced by Vaccination predisposes to affections of the respiratory organs. None who have acquaintance with the poor can have failed to observe how frequently the Bronchitis and Pneumonia of their children have been preceded by Vaccination—often occasioned, no doubt, by waiting and exposure at public vaccination stations.

Similar reasoning applies to other infantile ailments. It is not said they are caused by Vaccination, but that Vaccination contributes to their fatality. An infant that would have survived Bronchitis dies of Bronchitis *and* Vaccination ; dies of Teething *and* Vaccination ; dies of Convulsions *and* Vaccination ; dies of Whooping-Cough *and* Vaccination; and so on and on. We have no doubt whatever that were Vaccination abolished, the event would be immediately signalised by a great decrease of infant mortality.

The position of Anti-Vaccinists on the ground thus defined is perfectly intelligible and consistent with pathological science, and can only be brought into ridicule when misunderstood or misrepresented.

It is therefore vain to assert that conjunctions of the Vaccine Disease, and the debility consequent on Vaccine

Disease, with other diseases "are very rarely fatal." It is a statement which Sir Lyon Playfair wishes to have taken for true, but which is contrary to experience and incredible in itself.

The reference to the "expensive Return" of the Registrar General, No. 433, Session 1877, moved for by Mr. Hopwood, conducts to a remarkable confirmation of the increase of infant mortality coincident with more thorough Vaccination; and the reference to the Return is remarkable, as hitherto a dead silence has been maintained toward it by the medical profession and the press. The general public little imagine how the credit of Vaccination is maintained by the reserve designated "judicious." This hitherto unmentionable Return gave the number of deaths from fifteen specified diseases, which are inoculable or intensified by Vaccination. The following is a summary of the results—

```
Prior to Vaccination Acts—1847-53—
    Infants Died, 1847,  -    -    -    -    -    -    62,619
              Out of a population of 17,927,609.
Vaccination Obligatory—1854-67—
    Infants Died, 1854,  -    -    -    -    -    -    73,000
    Do.       1867,  -    -    -    -    -    -    92,827
              Out of a population of 20,066,224.
Vaccination Enforced—1868-75—
    Infants Died, 1868,  -    -    -    -    -    -    96,282
    Do.       1875,  -    -    -    -    -    -    106,173
              Out of a population of 22,712,266.
```

Thus, while the population of England had increased from 18 millions to 23 millions, the deaths of infants from 15 diseases had risen, in the same period, from 63,000 to 106,000. Had the mortality kept pace with the population, the deaths in 1875 would have been only 80,000; that is to say, in 1875 there perished in England 26,000 infants who would have lived had Vaccination remained as little in vogue as in 1847!

The result though startling in the gross is precisely what might have been foreseen and predicted. The infancy of a country cannot be systematically diseased, that is vaccinated, without exciting and aggravating other illnesses, and thereby enlarging the harvest of death.

The same Return reveals another noteworthy fact. Out of 80,000 deaths from Smallpox no less than 43,000 were under five years of age, at the very time when the effects of Vaccination were recent and potent in the blood !

We are asked, "Who would forbid the use of anæsthetics, or narcotics, or of drinking water, since these are at times occasions of death ;" but what comparison is there between such uses and risks, to which under circumstances we are compelled, and a wilful act like Vaccination ? When Inoculation with Smallpox was introduced by Maitland in 1721, the Rev. Edward Massey preached a sermon against the practice, which led to a controversy ; and in a letter Massey thus addressed Maitland—

"Inoculation, in your sense, is an engraftment of a corrupted body into a sound one ; an attempt to give a man a disease, who is in perfect health, which disease may prove mortal.

"This I said was tempting Providence.

"To which you reply, It resembles that of a person who leaps out of a window for fear of fire ; and surely that can never be reckoned a mistrust of Providence.

"No, certainly, Sir, if his house be really on fire, and the stairs burnt. 'Tis the only probable way of safety left ; and if the leap should kill him, the action could neither be called sinful or imprudent. But what should we say to a man who jumped out of the window when his house was not a-fire, only to try what he might perhaps be forced to do hereafter? This mad action exactly hits the case between us. For if my house be not on fire, that is, if I am in no apparent danger, what need I jump out of the window? What occasion is there to inoculate me?

"To carry on your own allegory, I would ask you, Sir, what human or divine authority you have to set a man's house on fire, that is, put a man who is in perfect health in danger of his life by a fit of illness? His own consent is not sufficient, because he has no more lawful power over his own life or health than you have, to put either of them in hazard."

Substitute Vaccination for Inoculation, and Massey's argument holds good as ever.

VI.—THE ASSERTED MITIGATION OF SMALLPOX.

"I pass to the second postulate of the Hon. Member " for Leicester—that Vaccination is no protection against " Smallpox. Do not forget what is the nature of the " disease against which we seek protection. Sir Thomas " Watson describes it in a few words as 'the most " 'hideous, loathsome, disfiguring, and probably, except " ' Hydrophobia, the most fatal also of the various diseases " 'to which the human body is liable.' Against this " mutilative and hideous disease we seek to erect barriers " by Vaccination. Individually, persons, since the time " of Jenner, protected themselves. The amount of pro- " tection, even by its discoverer, was thought to be " equivalent—but no more than equivalent to that of an " attack of Smallpox. In most cases, when men have had " Measles, Scarlatina, or Smallpox, they are protected " from future attacks, but not invariably, for there are " some persons who are subject to more than one attack. " In the call of the House of Lords to the Royal College " of Physicians to report to Parliament on the whole " subject of Vaccination, this liability is stated in express " terms. This Report is dated 1807, or nine years after " Jenner had published his discovery. The words are— " 'Where Smallpox has succeeded, it has been neither " 'the same in violence nor in the duration of its symp- " 'toms, but has, with very few exceptions, been remark- " 'ably mild, as if the Smallpox had been deprived by " 'the previous Vaccine Disease of all its usual malignity.' " That is precisely the state of our knowledge now, so

" that it is no discovery of the Anti-Vaccinators that
" there are cases of post-vaccinal Smallpox."

Whilst we have no desire to minimise the miseries
and mischiefs of Smallpox, there is no reason why they
should be magnified. With all respect for Sir Thomas
Watson, his words were wild words. The worst characteristics of Smallpox are specified as its ordinary
characteristics. To assert that with the exception of
Hydrophobia, it is probably the most fatal of diseases,
merely illustrates the frenzy with which it has become
the mode to speak of Smallpox. Against such extravagance we may set the observation of Sydenham, " If no
mischief be done either by physician or nurse, Smallpox
is the most slight and safe of all diseases." It is an
illusion that Smallpox became a mild disease consequent
on the introduction of Vaccination. It was a mild and
it was a severe disease a century ago and two centuries
ago as it is at this day. Dr. Wagstaffe, physician to St.
Bartholomew's Hospital, stated the fact accurately in
1722, when he wrote—

"There is scarcely, I believe, so great a difference between any two
distempers in the world as between the best and the worst sort of Smallpox in respect to the dangers which attend them. So true is that common
observation, that there is one sort in which a nurse cannot kill, and another
which even a physician cannot cure."

As Sir Lyon Playfair says—

" There are three varieties of Smallpox which repre-
" sent themselves in epidemics. The first is discrete
" Smallpox, where the pustules are separate and discrete,
" and it is rarely fatal. Then comes the confluent
" Smallpox where the pustules run together. In this
" form nearly half, or 50 per cent., of the Unvaccinated
" die. Of the Vaccinated when attacked, 15 per cent.
" die. Thirdly, comes the black or malignant form

" which rarely attacks the Vaccinated, but when it does
" it proves as fatal to them as to the Unvaccinated, for
" 95 per cent. of the persons attacked by this form of
" Smallpox die.   It rarely visits this country now in an
" epidemic form, but it did appear in a marked manner
" in the epidemics of 1871-2, and the London epidemic
" of 1881."

We shall have something to say about the Vaccinated
and Unvaccinated presently, and would now only point
out that the great majority of cases of Smallpox are
included in the first or discrete variety of Smallpox,
which, as said, *is rarely fatal;* which variety, we apprehend, was the form of the disease with which Sydenham
was familiar, and was therefore described by him as "the
most slight and safe of all diseases."

Thus defined, we escape from the haze of horror in
which Smallpox is invested.   Tissot, the famous Swiss
physician (born 1728—died 1797), writing in pre-
vaccination times, said—

"Epidemics of Smallpox, slight and severe, give a mortality of about
13 per cent., or 1 death out of 8 attacked."

Hospital Smallpox naturally gave a larger mortality.
Jurin, in 1723, cited 17,151 cases with 2,848 deaths, or
16.6 per cent.; and Duvillard 24,594 cases between
1700 and 1763 with 4,635 deaths, or 18.85 per cent.   In
Dr. Seaton's *Handbook of Vaccination* we read—

"From returns made to the Epidemiological Society in 1852, by 156
medical practitioners in various parts of England who had kept numerical
records of their Smallpox experience, it appeared that the proportion of
deaths to cases which they had met with in the natural form of the disease
was 19.7 per cent., or as nearly as possible 1 in 5."

The evidence thus tendered to the Epidemiological Society has to be qualified by the consideration that the
Unvaccinated in the years prior to 1852 had become a

section of the population discriminated from those in better conditions of life, who were Vaccinated. Anyhow, we discover that the mortality of Smallpox prior to Vaccination, or without Vaccination, ranged from 13 to 20 per cent.—a fact to be firmly borne in mind.

It is said that whilst Vaccination does not always prevent Smallpox, it makes it milder, and the report of the Royal College of Physicians in 1807 is cited in proof; but it is forgotten that in the report the Physicians were letting themselves down from their original asseveration, that Vaccination was an absolute preventive of Smallpox. When it is said that Vaccination modifies Smallpox and makes it milder, we ask, How do you know? Unless it could be ascertained how fierce Smallpox would be in a specified case without Vaccination, how can you tell how much milder it is with Vaccination? Something is predicated where demonstration is unattainable. It is said we cannot refute a prophet, but we may disbelieve him; and we utterly disbelieve that Smallpox is made milder by Vaccination. It is a statement for which in no single instance can there be a vestige of evidence. As shown, mild cases were common before Vaccination was heard of, and what made them mild? In the epidemic of 1870-72 there were admitted into the Metropolitan Asylums 14,808 cases of Smallpox, of whom 11,174 were Vaccinated, and 2,764 died. How much milder did Vaccination make Smallpox for the 2,764 who died?

It is also said that Vaccination was thought by Jenner to be "a protection from Smallpox equivalent to an attack of Smallpox, but no more than equivalent." Jenner, however, got his money on a very different undertaking, namely—

"That the human frame when *once* it has felt the influence of the genuine Cowpox, *is never afterwards*, at any period of its existence, assailable by Smallpox."

Smallpox after Smallpox is far from uncommon, but the assertion that the phenomenon is comparable in frequency with Smallpox after Vaccination is unworthy of discussion. That it should have been advanced by Sir William Gull and then by Sir Lyon Playfair is another illustration of the recklessness with which anything that is supposed to make for the glory of Vaccination is asserted.

———

VII.—THE GRAND 3000 PER MILLION STATISTIC.

" In examining the state of Vaccination, we must " compare the Mortality from Smallpox with that of last " century. This, Dr. Farr tells us, was 3000 per million " of the population annually for the whole country."

Let us pay special attention to this statistic because of the importance assigned to it, and because it affords an excellent test of Sir Lyon Playfair's veracity.

First, we ask, Where does Dr. Farr tell us "that the Mortality from Smallpox was 3000 per million for the whole country last century?" It would not be safe to meet the statement with a direct negative, for Dr. Farr may somewhere have been betrayed into a thoughtless repetition of the fiction; but it is unlikely, and therefore we ask, Where?

At a session of the Vaccination Committee on 7th March, 1871, Dr. Lyon Playfair being present, the 3000 per million statistic was under consideration, and Dr. C. T. Pearce stated—

"I put the question to Dr. Farr at Somerset House whether the estimate of 3000 per million was to be relied upon, and whether there were any statistics that would enable such a conclusion to be arrived at; and Dr. Farr said emphatically, 'No, it is a mere estimate; no statistics of the last century, or of the previous one, are to be relied upon.'"

Dr. Farr's answer to Dr. Pearce was matter of course. There are no trustworthy statistics for last century or for the first third of the present. The 3000 per million Smallpox Mortality was never more than a conjectural estimate; and it is easy to show that as a conjectural estimate it is preposterous.

It originated thus. Dr. Lettsom in his *Observations on the Cowpox*, published in 1801, during the early Vaccination furore, wrote—

" In London and its environs there are about one million of inhabitants, of whom about 3000 die annually by the natural Smallpox, or about 36,000 in Great Britain and Ireland."

Dr. Lettsom's estimate was raised by Sir Gilbert Blane to 45,000, and, fancy being free, other estimates were put forth, and continue to be put forth; Dr. Playfair himself saying at St. Mary's Hospital in 1870, that "80,000 lives were saved annually by Vaccination."

But did 3000 die annually of Smallpox in London last century? Fortunately we can refer to Dr. Farr for an answer. In M'Culloch's *Statistical Account of the British Empire* he wrote—

" Smallpox attained its maximum mortality after Inoculation was introduced. The annual deaths from Smallpox averaged 2323 from 1760 to 1779; in the next twenty years they declined to 1740; this disease, therefore, began to grow less fatal before Vaccination was discovered; indicating, together with the diminution of Fever, the general improvement in health then taking place."

Thus the average annual London Smallpox mortality toward the close of last century was not 3000: it was 1740.

But whatever the metropolitan death-rate, where was the warrant for converting it into the death-rate of England, Wales, Scotland and Ireland? London overcrowded and pestiferous, was no standard for the general population, urban or rural; and the assumption was monstrous that Smallpox, a notoriously sporadic disease, was constant and equally diffused over the land. We are without statistics for the time in question, but arguing from London of to-day in constant communication with the provinces, to London of the 18th century in comparative isolation, what do we find? Why, Smallpox prevalent in London with little or no Smallpox in the country! In tne early part of 1878 there were 1,134 fatal cases registered within fifteen miles of Charing Cross, while but 8 occurred in nineteen English towns with an aggregate population equal to that of London. Indeed, forgetful of its destruction of his own case, Sir Lyon Playfair brings out the irregularity between London and country Smallpox in forcible terms. Thus he says—

" The epidemic of 1871 struck the civil population of
" England and Wales strongly *and was exceptionally*
" *severe in the metropolis.* With the exception of local
" outbursts in Birmingham, Liverpool, and Salford,
" Smallpox since 1873 has been very small in all our
" large towns, *except London,* where it has lingered, and
" came as a renewed outburst in 1877 and 1881. Most
" of the arguments of the Anti-Vaccinators are derived
" from Metropolitan Smallpox. Thus, in 1880 the
" total deaths in England and Wales from Smallpox
" were 648, *out of which London alone was responsible for*
" *471.* The epidemic of 1871-72 was general and severe,
" but the recent epidemics of 1877 and 1881 *have been*
" *mainly Metropolitan.* . . . While, therefore, other
" parts of the country seem to have recovered from the

" great epidemic influence of 1871, *London has not yet*
" *gained control over the disease.* It had practical im-
" munity in 1873, 74, 75, but outbursts came in 1877 and
" 1881—in the latter year to about one-third of the
" extent of 1871, but still amounting to 640 per million.
" That, large as it is, represents about one-fifth of the
" average mortality of the last century. *The other parts*
" *of England and Wales during the same year had only a*
" *mortality of 100 per million.*"

The sporadic character of Smallpox is illustrated where-
ever we get at the figures. In 1874 there were in London
735 deaths from Smallpox but not one in Birmingham;
386 in Liverpool, but not one in Plymouth; 347 in Salford, but not one in Nottingham; 190 in Manchester,
and but 1 in Sheffield; 24 in Bristol and 4 in Leeds; and
so on. What reason is there to believe that what is true
of Smallpox within our own experience was otherwise
than true in the experience of our forefathers?

With these facts before us, we see how baseless was
Lettsom's original estimate, and how unwarrantable was
the extension of the London rate to the population of
the United Kingdom, and the assumption of the equal
diffusion of the disease over the country. Yet the imaginary statistic is used by Sir Lyon Playfair as if its accuracy were indisputable—eking it out occasionally with
an exaggeration of his own; thus—

" The average death-rate from Smallpox in London
" before Vaccination *was 4,000 per million*, and in the
" great epidemic year 1871, it was 2,420 per million. So
" that even in this exceptionally severe epidemic the
" death-rate was only about one-half of that of average
" years in last century."

Dr. Lettsom said the London Smallpox death-rate

was 3000 per million; Dr. Farr said it had fallen to 1740 before Vaccination was introduced; whilst Sir Lyon Playfair says it was 4000. Well, statistics at discretion cost nothing, and are worth—what they cost.

VIII.—CHARITABLE VACCINATION—1801-40.

" For the first forty years of this century Vaccination
" was promoted among the people by charitable agencies,
" and Smallpox Mortality had fallen to 600 per million
" by 1840, or was then only one-fifth the amount of last
" century."

Having knocked off the 3000 per million imposition, the preceding statement loses much of its impressiveness. What remains is equally factitious, but before dealing with details, it may be useful to interpose a few words on the fall in Smallpox which marked the close of last century and the opening of the present.

Dr. Farr observed that Smallpox was declining in London prior to the introduction of Vaccination, and the decline which he remarked was not limited to London. As to the cause of this decline, we can only conjecture. Sir Lyon Playfair offers an explanation, saying—

" Modern science tends to show that such diseases
" as Smallpox arise from the growth in the blood of
" minute organisms. Now, like other crops, there are
" good and bad years for their growth. Just as there
" are good years for pears, apples, and plums, so there
" are good years for Smallpox, Measles, and Scarlatina.
" In the case of Smallpox, these good years come every
" fourth or fifth year, and then the crops are good or
" excessive."

Another and more comprehensive explanation is that of Dr. Hamernik, who says—

" Even as many individuals of the animal and vegetable kingdoms have disappeared, so also have great changes taken place in the number and severity of diseases. When Scurvy, Putrid Fevers, Dysentery, etc., were commoner, Smallpox was likely to be more malignant : so much was due to the prevalent poverty and scarcity throughout Europe. Pauperism, want, and hunger are always characterised by a proportionate frequency, gravity, and diffusion of various diseases."

The decline in Smallpox which preceded and accompanied the introduction of Vaccination is strikingly illustrated in the case of Vienna. Jenner and his friends made an extraordinary fuss over the extinction of Smallpox in that city according to the following table—

Years.	Total Deaths.			From Smallpox.		
1791-1800 average	14,600	...	...	835	or one in	17½
1801	... 15,181	...	...	164	...	93
1802	... 14,522	...	...	61	...	238
1803	... 14,383	...	...	27	...	532
1804	... 14,035	...	...	2	...	7,017

Yet it was never pretended that from 1801 to 1804 more than an insignificant fraction of the Viennese were vaccinated. De Carro was one of the earliest and most enthusiastic of Jenner's followers. Eager to vaccinate, he was for a time prohibited. Nevertheless, he reported in the *Medical and Physical Journal*, vol. x. p. 243, under date 10th June, 1803—

" In Vienna we no longer hear of Smallpox. For these two years and a half, I have not met with a single instance of it, and many other physicians will say the same."

The early victories ascribed to Vaccination were victories either over an imaginary or a retreating enemy, as we see in the case of Vienna. We cannot too firmly insist upon this point in presence of the claim continually

advanced for the subjugation of Smallpox consequent
on the introduction of Vaccination. From some cause
undefined, and, probably in its full extent undiscoverable,
a subsidence of Smallpox over Europe set in toward the
close of last century, and continued throughout the first
part of the present ; and to this subsidence the favour
that Vaccination met with was largely due. The decline
in the disease concurrently with the introduction of
Vaccination, was ascribed to Vaccination, although the
decline prevailed among an overwhelming majority who
had never received Vaccination. To make good the
claim for Vaccination it would be necessary to maintain
that the rite, as applied to 2 or 3 per cent. of Europeans,
effected the salvation of 98 or 97 per cent.

Returning to Charitable Vaccination, we have first to
observe that Sir Lyon Playfair's Smallpox statistics are
London statistics down to 1840—the national registration of deaths commencing in 1837. Following Lettsom,
he assumes London Smallpox as annually accountable
for 3000 deaths per million, and extends that rate of
mortality to the entire population of the United Kingdom—a fallacious proceeding sufficiently exposed. He
then goes on to represent that the said 3000 per million
was reduced by Charitable Vaccination to 600 per million
by 1840, "or one fifth of the amount of last century"—
still identifying London Smallpox with National Smallpox, the latter, as said, being undefined until after
1837.

Considering the figures manipulated are based on the
London bills of mortality, it will be interesting to refer
to those bills and see how far they were affected by
Charitable Vaccination during the years in question.

DEATHS FROM SMALLPOX WITHIN THE LONDON BILLS OF
MORTALITY—1801-40.

1801—1461	1811— 751	1821— 508	1831— 563
2—1579	12—1287	22— 604	32— 771
3—1202	13— 898	23— 774	33— 574
4— 622	14— 638	24— 725	34— 334
5—1685	15— 725	25—1299	35— 863
6—1158	16— 653	26— 503	36— 536
7—1297	17—1051	27— 616	37— 217
8—1169	18— 421	28— 598	38— 788
9—1163	19— 712	29— 736	39— 239
10—1198	20— 792	30— 627	40— 231
Total—12,534	7928	6990	5116

With these figures before us, we ask where is the
evidence of the progressive influence of Charitable Vaccination in reducing the mortality of Smallpox from
3000 to 600 per million ? Vaccination was most extensively practised in London during the first decade—
1801-10, when there was most Smallpox ; but its manifest failure to prevent Smallpox, with the injury and
death which followed the practice, brought it into disrepute. Hence there were far fewer Vaccinations effected
in London in the subsequent thirty years, 1811-40, whilst
none the less did Smallpox keep falling off until the
outbreak of the severe epidemic of 1838-40, represented
with startling difference in the bills of mortality and in
the larger London brought within systematic registration in 1838. Thus—

LONDON WITHIN BILLS OF MORTALITY.		LONDON ACCORDING TO REGISTRAR-GENERAL.	
Years.	Deaths from Smallpox.	Years.	Deaths from Smallpox.
1838	788	1838	3817
1839	239	1839	634
1840	231	1840	1235
Total,	1258	Total,	5686

Prior to 1838, Smallpox statistics outside certain

3

localities are matter of inference and conjecture, and, so far as based on the London bills of mortality, are necessarily illusory. Subsequent to 1837, we have the Registrar-General's returns to refer to, and come upon firmer ground—ground which we cannot too carefully separate from the region on the other side, where amid uncertainties conjurers disport themselves.

It is said Charitable Vaccination reduced Smallpox Mortality from 3000 to 600 per million between 1801 and 1840. The imaginary 3000 per million has been disposed of, but what of the 600? Well, a heavy figure being wanted to start from, it is conveniently supplied by the great epidemic of 1838-40, coinciding with the commencement of registration. In that epidemic 35,833 died in England and Wales, giving a death-rate of 1,101 per million in 1838, of 604 in 1839, and of 679 in 1840. There is no reason, however, but the contrary, to suppose that rates anything like these prevailed in non-epidemic years from the beginning of the century.

IX.—Gratuitous Vaccination—1841-53.

" Still, 600 per million is a high rate of mortality, and
" Parliament began in 1841 to give funds for Gratuitous
" Vaccination, so as to spread it more rapidly among
" the people. This continued till 1853, and the mortality
" was now 305 per million, so that Gratuitous Vaccina-
" tion of the State reduced the mortality to one-half."

An Act was passed in 1840 enabling Poor Law Guardians to provide and pay for Vaccination out of the poor rate ; and consequent on that Act, we are told by Sir Lyon Playfair, the Smallpox Mortality of 600 per million was reduced to 305 per million in 1853. Of course if the Act of 1840 had the influence asserted, it would be a progressive influence, reducing Smallpox from year to year. Wherefore let us see whether such progressive reduction is apparent in the returns of the Registrar-General. Here is his statement for the years in question —from 1841 to 1853 inclusive—

Year.	Population.	Deaths from all Causes.	Deaths from Smallpox.	Deaths from Smallpox per million of Population.
1841 ...	15,929,492 ...	343,847 ...	6,368 ...	408
42 ...	16,123,793 ...	349,519 ...	2,715 ...	172
43 ⎫ 44 ⎪ 45 ⎬ 46 ⎭		The causes of death were not analysed by the Registrar-General for these years.		
47 ...	17,131,512 ...	420,304 ...	4,227 ...	246
48 ...	17,340,492 ...	398,531 ...	6,903 ...	398
49 ...	17,552,020 ...	440,839 ...	4,644 ...	264
50 ...	17,766,129 ...	368,995 ...	4,665 ...	263
51 ...	17,982,849 ...	395,396 ...	6,997 ...	396
52 ...	18,205,627 ...	407,135 ...	7,320 ...	409
53 ...	18,403,313 ...	421,097 ...	3,151 ...	174

Where, we ask, is the progressive decrease manifest in these figures? To Charitable Vaccination, says Sir Lyon Playfair, was adjoined Gratuitous Vaccination by the State in 1841, which reduced Smallpox Mortality by one half—from 600 per million in 1840 to 302 or 305 in 1853. But whilst it is an unwarrantable assumption that 600 per million was the prevalent rate prior to the great epidemic of 1838-40, it is obvious to anyone who examines the Registrar-General's returns, 1841-53, that Gratuitous Vaccination by the State did not effect the progressive reduction asserted, or had any appreciable influence whatever on the National Smallpox.

Lord Lyttelton, speaking in the House of Lords on 12th April, 1853, in advocacy of enforced Vaccination, endeavoured to justify the project by showing how irregular was the observance of Vaccination throughout the country. He said—

"We are told that the number of births registered in England and Wales in the year ending September 29th, 1852, was 601,839, and the number vaccinated during that period under the Vaccination Act was 397,128; so that, in round numbers, 400,000 were vaccinated by the machinery in force, leaving only 200,000, or one-third of the whole number, to be treated in the numerous Private Vaccinations which took place. There are several important fallacies in that statement. That general result is by no means the consequence of anything like a uniform system throughout the country. I have before me a detailed statement of the extent of Vaccination in various parts of England in 1851, which shows that there is great want of uniformity in certain districts. In towns where the people have a shorter distance to go to get their children vaccinated, the result is more favourable than in the rural districts. For example, in Birmingham, on the total number of births in the year 1851 the Vaccinations were 91 per cent.; in Leicester they were 41 per cent.; and in Loughborough only 18 per cent. The contrast between the manufacturing and the rural districts is favourable on the side of the former. In Bideford, the Vaccinations were only 11 per cent. upon the births; in West Ashford, in Kent, they were only 22 per cent.; and in Winchcomb only 6 per cent. While the general average, however, is lower in the agricultural than in the manufacturing districts, some contrary instances are found. Thus in Derby the Vaccinations are only 42 per cent., while at Watford, which is a rural district, the Vaccinations were 126 per cent. upon the births in 1851. That included, of course, the Vaccination of children born in previous years. But in London, and in no less a parish than that of St. James's, Westminster, it is reported that in 1851 on 973 births only 44 Vaccinations took place; while in Wellingborough Union, where there were 800 births in 1851, no Vaccination at all is reported!"

These details are noteworthy and instructive. Strange to say, Lord Lyttelton made no attempt to complete his argument. He ought to have shown that in the places where Vaccination was least practised there was most Smallpox, and where most practised there was least Smallpox. Had he made the attempt his eyes might have been opened, and the country saved from a cruel and costly infliction.

Lord Shaftesbury, in continuation, cited similar instances of neglected Vaccination as follows—

	Births, 1851.		Vaccinations.
Paddington	1,458	...	386
Hampstead	286	...	93
Huntingdon	805	...	68
St. Neots	671	...	17
Carnarvon	929	...	125
Bangor and Beaumaris	1,025	...	420
Newton Abbott	1,563	...	150

He, too, forgot to show that these places were "decimated" (that's the word) with Smallpox, whilst other places where Vaccination was generally practised enjoyed exemption. On the contrary, with curious inconsequence, he went on to recommend a sure pre· scription of his own, namely, improved dwellings for the poor. These were his words—

"It is perfectly true that Smallpox is chiefly confined to the lowest classes of the population ; and I believe *that with improved lodging-houses, the disease might be all but exterminated.*"

Not a doubt of it; but if improved lodging-houses would "all but exterminate Smallpox," why have gone on to waste labour and money on a superfluity like Vaccination?

X.—Obligatory Vaccination—1854-81.

" Then Parliament in 1853 passed an Obligatory Law, " which remained without administrative means of en- " forcing it till 1871 ; but still during this period of " Obligatory Vaccination, Smallpox Mortality fell to " 223 deaths per million. In that year a law was passed " making it compulsory on Boards of Guardians to " appoint Vaccination Officers, and since that time " the average Smallpox Mortality has been 156 per " million."

Thus, according to Sir Lyon Playfair, there never was a more docile subject than Smallpox. The waves are not ruled by Britannia with greater facility. Parliament has issued successive edicts, and straightway throughout

the land there are answering results—Smallpox falling
off with arithmetical precision. In these days of scepticism as to legislative omnipotence, it is singular to find
a confession of faith so naïve from a man of the world
whom years of experience might be supposed to have
hardened and disillusioned. Parliament capable of so
much might be capable of more; and having cut down
Smallpox might proceed to dispose of Scarlatina and
Measles, Diphtheria and Whooping-Cough, Typhus and
Typhoid in similar fashion; and thus Englishmen find
themselves enclosed in the realm of Hygeia before they
know it.

Such might be the natural inference from Sir Lyon's
buoyant exposition; but the exposition will not bear
examination. Not to mention other diseases, many
medical men entertain no expectation that Smallpox
can be exterminated, even with the aid of Vaccination.
In this opinion we do not share. Smallpox *is* exterminated in many sections of the community resident in
wholesome conditions; and there is nothing essential in
those conditions to prevent their extension to all sections. The time may not be distant when a case of
Smallpox will be accounted discreditable, and taken as
a sure index to some disorder demanding correction.

There is no better answer to Sir Lyon Playfair's statements relative to the influence of Obligatory Vaccination
than the exhibition of the returns of the Registrar-
General. It is asserted that under Obligatory Vaccination, and in proportion to its stringency, Vaccinations
increased, and that as they increased, Smallpox diminished. Was it so? Vaccination was made compulsory
under penalty of fine or imprisonment in 1853, and here

is the record of Vaccinations and Smallpox in England
and Wales for the subsequent 28 years, 1854-81, with
the preceding 3 years, 1851-53, to give it completeness,
copied from the 11th Annual Report of the Local
Government Board.

Years.	Population.	Successful Vaccinations at the expense of the Poor Rate.	Deaths from Smallpox in Decades.	Deaths from Smallpox.	Deaths from Smallpox per Million Pop.	Deaths from Smallpox. Annual Average for each five Years.
1851	17,982,849			6,997	396	
1852	18,193,206	397,128		7,320	409	
1853	18,404,368	366,593		3,151	174	253·6
1854	18,616,310	677,886		2,808	153	1851-55
1855	18,829,000	448,519	42,071 (10 yrs.) 1851-60	2,525	136	
1856	19,042,412	422,281		2,277	121	
1857	19,256,516	411,268		3,936	206	
1858	19,471,291	455,004		6,414	329	197·0
1859	19,686,701	445,020		3,798	193	1856-60
1860	19,902,713	485,927		2,713	136	
1861	20,119,314	425,739		1,290	64	
1862	20,371,013	437,693		1,579	78	
1863	20,625,855	646,464		5,891	286	218·8
1864	20,883,889	529,479		7,624	365	1861-65
1865	21,145,151	578,583	34,786 (10 yrs.) 1861-70	6,361	301	
1866	21,409,684	454,885		2,977	139	
1867	21,677,525	490,598		2,467	114	
1868	21,948,713	513,042		1,994	91	104·8
1869	22,223,299	524,143		1,482	67	1866-70
1870	22,501,316	472,881		2,547	113	
1871	22,788,466	693,104		23,062	1,012	
1872	23,095,819	669,320		19,022	824	
1873	23,407,317	501,189		2,303	98	411·4
1874	23,723,017	493,285		2,084	88	1871-75
1875	24,042,974	498,952	57,422 (10 yrs.) 1871-80	849	35	
1876	24,367,247	566,587		2,408	99	
1877	24,695,894	529,376		4,278	173	
1878	25,028,973	513,575		1,856	74	78·4
1879	25,366,544	519,715		536	21	1876-80
1880	25,708,666	513,283		648	25	
1881	26,055,406	533,005		3,098	119	

This record completely nullifies Sir Lyon Playfair's assumptions. When we inquire whence he derived his extraordinary statistics, we are referred to the following statement—

	Years.	Deaths from Smallpox per Million.	Periods.
VACCINATION OPTIONAL..........	1847-53	305	7 years.
VACCINATION OBLIGATORY (but not officially enforced).........	1854-71	223	18 years.
VACCINATION OBLIGATORY (and efficiently enforced by Vaccination Officers)...............	1872-80	156	9 years.

The figures are correct, but on what principle are the Periods arranged—7 years, 18 years, 9 years! The principle, it may be said, is the more or less efficient administration of Vaccination; but if we refer to the record of Vaccinations, we find no increase in their number (taking the augmentation of population into account) answering to the specified access of severity in the law. By this arrangement, too, the extraordinary epidemic of 1871-72 (when 42,084 died) is split in two—the mortality of 1871 (when 23,062 died) being diluted in the mortality of 17 preceding years in order to magnify the contrast with the mortality of the 9 succeeding years! It is plain that statistics thus handled may be shaped and varied to any desired conclusion. "Cookery" that would be accounted fraudulent in finance, acquires another character when undertaken for the glory of Vaccination. "Deceit," it has been said, "is good or evil according to the purpose for which we deceive"; and what purpose can be more praiseworthy than the preservation of mankind from Smallpox!

XI.—SUMMARY OF ASSERTION AND CONTRADICTION.

" Thus every successive step in promoting Vaccination
" has been followed by a great reduction in the rate of
" Smallpox Mortality. Voluntary efforts reduced the
" Mortality of the last Century from 3000 to 600 per
" million ; Gratuitous Vaccination by the State reduced
" it to 302, and Obligatory Law inefficiently administered
" reduced it to 223, and the same law under Vaccination
" Officers further reduces it to 156. That is the general
" result as regards England and Wales."

Such is Sir Lyon Playfair's summary. Our answer in
summary is, that the asserted cause of the reduction of
Smallpox is illusory, and that the successive steps of the
reduction are contrived to make plausible the original
illusion, and have no true correspondence with realities :
That the Smallpox Mortality of England and Wales
during last century was 3000 per million is an unwarrantable conjecture : That 600 per million in 1838-41 did
not represent *a reduced* but *an enlarged* mortality consequent on the severest epidemic of the present century :
And that the progressive reduction of Smallpox effected
by the progressive extension and enforcement of Vaccination is a wilful attempt to substitute what is considered
ought to be true for what *is true.*

At the same time, we are not concerned to deny that
we are less troubled with Smallpox than our forefathers.
Smallpox flourishes in insanitary conditions of life, and
we therefore expect the disease to diminish in so far as
sanitary conditions have prevailed. Mr. J. Russell
Lowell, in his discourse upon Fielding at Taunton,
observed—

"We must guard against the anachronism of forgetting the coarseness of the age in which Fielding was born, and whose atmosphere he breathed. It was a generation whose sense of smell was undisturbed by odours that would now evoke a sanitary commission, and its moral nostrils were of an equally masculine temper."

That it was a generation whose sense of smell was undisturbed by odours that would now evoke a sanitary commission is a fact not to be forgotten ; in connection with which we may recall Dr. Alfred Carpenter's observation, that if people would clear away from their habitations those matters which evolve evil odours, they would get rid of Smallpox and might dispense with Vaccination— indifference to such odours, therefore, accounting for the Smallpox which afflicted the eighteenth century just as similar indifference accounts for Smallpox in this.

It is sometimes pointed out with triumph that in the 5 years, 1876-80, the Smallpox death-rate declined to 78 per million, the lowest of the century ; but inasmuch as Vaccination was no more extensively practised in those years than in 1871-75 when the rate was 411 per million, it is vain to ascribe the reduced rate to Vaccination. We have to bear in mind that the years of 411 per million were preceded by 5 years, 1866-70, of 104 per million, for which Vaccination had the credit, none foreseeing the epidemic ahead in which Vaccination proved powerless.

The epidemic years 1838-42, when the Smallpox Mortality of England and Wales was 576 per million, were likewise preceded by a low death-rate from the disease. Thus in London we find the figures registered—

Years.			Deaths from Smallpox.	Years.			Deaths from Smallpox.
1834	...	...	334	1838	...	...	3,817
1835	...	...	863	1839	...	...	634
1836	...	...	536	1840	...	...	1,235
1837	...	...	217	1841	...	...	1,053

We have also to note, that in the great epidemic of 1838-40, when 35,833 perished in England and Wales, the population was not vaccinated to the extent of 50 per cent., nine-tenths of the lower classes, constituting the vast majority of the sufferers, being unvaccinated. In the corresponding epidemic of 1871-72, when 42,084 perished, it was claimed that the population was vaccinated to the extent of 95 per cent.; and what difference did the Vaccination make? Any difference for good would be amply accounted for by improved conditions of life, yet the mortality per million was considerably higher in the latter than in the former epidemic—918 per million in the 2 years, 1871-72, to 772 per million in the 3 years 1838-40.

Whilst theorists like Sir Lyon Playfair romance about the reduction and extermination of Smallpox by means of Vaccination, yet when men are brought into practical relation with the disease, their behaviour assumes a different fashion, and what faith they have in the Jennerian rite proves to be like much other faith—a form of make-believe never intended for serious use. Thus Dr. Ballard, of the Local Government Board, does not hesitate to extinguish the fond expectation of exterminated Smallpox in these unequivocal terms—

"Experience has not verified Jenner's prediction. Smallpox has not been eradicated. Let me add that scientific observation and reasoning give no countenance to the belief that it ever will be eradicated from civilised communities."

Again a Royal Commission was appointed in 1881 to inquire respecting the provision of Smallpox Hospitals for London, and in their report the Commissioners observe:—

"The amount of Metropolitan Mortality from Smallpox is strangely irregular, ranging from 2,422 per million in 1871 to 13 in 1875. The population of London will soon be 4,000,000, and if we assume for the moment that the past 43 years, 1838-80, is our best measure of the future, it would seem that we have to expect once in about 30 years an absolute mortality varying from 8,000 to 10,000 deaths, and apart from these extraordinary outbursts, that the sickness of the remaining 41 years will be indicated by a mortality ranging in 3 years from 2,800 to 3,000, in 17 years from 1,000 to 2,800, in 13 years from 400 to 1,000, and in 8 years under 400—"

The conclusion being that hospital accommodation is requisite for 2,700 Londoners smitten with Smallpox. That is to say, the Royal Commissioners distinctly contemplate the occurrence of epidemics in London in which for 2,700 patients it will be necessary to provide beds. Could surrender of the efficacy of Vaccination be more complete? The Commission consisted of fervent Vaccinists, not one of whom would hesitate to stand up for Vaccination through thick and thin. The Commissioners had a population to deal with practically vaccinated to the level of the birth-rate; the entire public service revaccinated, with a multitude of the young and the fearful, and all prisoners; and yet for a population thus protected it is necessary to have beds in readiness for 2,700 victims! With Vaccination preached in every newspaper, advertised at every church door, and offered gratis; with gangs of public vaccinators stimulated with fees and extra awards; with vaccination officers to hunt up the careless and recalcitrant like sleuth-hounds; with the terrors of the police-court and fines and imprisonment; yet it is all in vain! London is open as ever to an invasion of Smallpox, and mercy and prudence demand the provision of 2,700 beds! Imagine Jenner who proclaimed Smallpox exterminated in the chief capitals of Europe, and dissipated like chaff in the vast empires of Asia and America, foreseeing such an issue !

XII.—SMALLPOX AND VACCINATION IN SCOTLAND AND IRELAND.

"Scotland and Ireland did not get a compulsory law " till 1863, or ten years later than England. In the next " ten years there were two years of a very heavy epi- " demic, but still the average Smallpox Mortality of this " decade was 214 per million in Scotland, and only 108 " in Ireland. From 1875 to 1882 the rate in Ireland has " been only 72 per million, and is scarcely measurable " in Scotland, for it is only 6 per million."

"Smallpox Mortality," say the Royal Commissioners, referring to London, " is strangely irregular, ranging from 2,422 per million in 1871 to 13 in 1875 ;" and what is true of Smallpox in London is equally true of Smallpox in Scotland and Ireland. In Sir Lyon Playfair's own words, " Just as there are good years for pears, apples, and plums, so there are good years for Smallpox." Such being the habit of the malady, where is the sense of ascribing years of little Smallpox to the effect of Vaccination and years of much Smallpox to the defect of Vaccination, when in all the years Vaccination is equal ? It is claimed that in recent years Smallpox has been almost extinct in Scotland, but in the years prior to the great epidemic of 1871-72 the like subsidence of the disease was observed, and it was proudly assumed that Vaccination had done its work and made an end of Smallpox. Dr. Wood, President of the Royal College of Physicians, Edinburgh, testifying before the Vaccination Committee 1871, said—

"Since the Compulsory Vaccination Act there is a decided diminution of Smallpox. In fact, *we have had no epidemic of Smallpox in Scotland* since the Vaccination Act of 1863."

And in reply to another question, Dr. Wood said—

"The operation of the Act of 1863 has *very largely diminished the amount of epidemic Smallpox in Scotland.*"

It was the same in Ireland. The Act of 1863 was followed by a subsidence of Smallpox, and Vaccination had the credit, Sir Dominic Corrigan, M.D., testifying before the Vaccination Committee to the same tune as did Dr. Wood of Scotland. And Dr. Lyon Playfair, speaking in the House of Commons, 6th July, 1870, said—

"There cannot be the least doubt that Compulsory Vaccination Laws when properly applied as in Scotland and Ireland, are perfectly equal to stamp out Smallpox in any country—"

Which was to say that Smallpox had been by such legislation stamped out in Scotland and in Ireland ; and speaking in 1870 there were appearances to justify the assertion. In 1869 there were 64 deaths from Smallpox in Scotland, and in 1868 only 15. In Ireland in 1869 there were 20 deaths, and in 1870 there were 32. But whatever the appearance, those who had studied Smallpox apart from the bewilderment of Vaccination were not deceived, and predicted confidently that Smallpox would return as an epidemic, which it straightway did in 1871-72, to the confusion of the cowpox soothsayers and those who had placed their trust in them. The state of the case will be best understood if we set before us the Smallpox Mortality of both countries for seventeen years following the Compulsory Vaccination Acts—

SCOTLAND.			IRELAND.		
Years.		Deaths from Smallpox.	Years.		Deaths from Smallpox.
1864,	... ...	1,741	1864,	... ...	854
1865,	... ...	383	1865,	... ...	461
1866,	... ...	200	1866,	... ...	194
1867,	... ...	100	1867,	... ...	21
1868,	... ...	15	1868,	... ...	23
1869,	... ...	64	1869,	... ...	20
1870,	... ...	114	1870,	... ...	32
1871,	... ...	1,442	1871,	... ...	665
1872,	... ...	2,466	1872,	... ...	3,248
1873,	... ...	1,126	1873,	... ...	504
1874,	... ...	1,246	1874,	... ...	569
1875,	... ...	76	1875,	... ...	535
1876,	... ...	39	1876,	... ...	24
1877,	... ...	38	1877,	... ...	71
1878,	... ...	4	1878,	... ...	873
1879,	... ...	8	1879,	... ...	672
1880,	... ...	10	1880,	... ...	389

Who, considering these figures, can draw from them the conclusion Sir Lyon Playfair tries to enforce? Scotland and Ireland are alike fully vaccinated, the natives being equally credulous and submissive; yet Smallpox appears and disappears, Vaccination being a thing irrelevant.

XIII.—SMALLPOX STAMPED OUT IN SCOTLAND, 1870.

"My Hon. Friend the member for Stockport (Mr.
" C. H. Hopwood), both in and out of Parliament, points
" to the epidemic of 1871-3 in Scotland as a refutation
" of what he deems a supremely silly remark of mine,
" that the Vaccination Act in Scotland was sufficient to
" stamp Smallpox out of that country. That is exactly
" what it has done. The words 'stamp out' are
" borrowed from the Cattle Plague Commission, of which
" I was a member. The Cattle Plague Commission
" thought that the measures recommended by them were
" sufficient to stamp out the disease, but not to keep it

" out ; for great epidemics are like huge tidal waves,
" which may roll over any ordinary embankments."

It is natural that Sir Lyon Playfair should feel irritated
by Mr. Hopwood's caustic observations on his proclamation in 1870 that the Vaccination Act had stamped out
Smallpox in Scotland—a proclamation that would never
have been uttered had the impending epidemic of
1871-73 been foreseen.   The defence of "the supremely
silly remark" intensifies its silliness, and save for over
confidence in his own plausibility the author of the
exploded prediction would have discreetly kept silence
and let bad alone.

The notion of stamping out Smallpox by Vaccination
is far older than the Cattle Plague Commission. Jenner
himself, in 1801, after asserting " That the human frame
when once it has felt the influence of the genuine Cowpox [namely, Horsegrease Cowpox] is never afterwards,
at any period of its existence, assailable by Smallpox,"
went on to congratulate his country—

"On beholding an antidote *that is capable of extirpating from the earth*
a disease which is every hour devouring its victims—a disease that has ever
been considered the severest scourge of the human race."

And in later years, when discredited and fretting in
neglect at Berkeley, he wrote, 12th October, 1812, of an
outbreak of Smallpox in London—

"Had I power to exercise Vaccination as I like, in one fortnight this
dismal work of death should entirely cease."

Thus Jenner held it possible to stamp out London
Smallpox in a fortnight ; and the miracle Jenner projected Dr. Martin, of Boston, habitually fulfils. At the
meeting of the British Medical Association at Ryde, in
1881, he assured his audience—

"I am called upon at times, at the very shortest notice, to vaccinate whole cities; and when I left America I had just completed the Vaccination of the city of New Haven. The custom now is to send for me, or for my son, whenever Smallpox breaks out, with orders to vaccinate the whole population of the city, town, or neighbourhood; and it is done immediately, the result being that an epidemic is completely stopped in a week."

Nor was this American Munchausen heard with scepticism: on the contrary, he was rewarded with rounds of applause, and his discourse reproduced in the *British Medical Journal*—anything being acceptable that makes for the glory of Vaccination.

In further proof of the existence of the expectation that Vaccination would exterminate Smallpox, we find in the *Medical and Physical Journal* for December, 1805, a correspondent writing from Edinburgh, as follows—

"Vaccination is here *universally adopted*. [The italics are the writer's.] A case of confluent Smallpox occurred in the hospital a few weeks since. Dr. Rutherford, the clinical professor, advised us to regard it rather as *a curiosity* than as a case of importance, *as we should probably not see another*.

"Dr. Gregory, when lecturing on Smallpox, observed that he should treat the subject very lightly, as he expected the disease would cease to exist in this country in a few years."

Sir Lyon Playfair has no need, therefore, to excuse himself as if responsible for the notion of stamping out Smallpox by means of Vaccination. He shares it with predecessors and contemporaries; and if put afresh to shame by an outbreak of Smallpox in Scotland, he may not perhaps disdain to justify his confidence by an appeal to the miracles of Dr. Martin.

XIV.—Smallpox a Flood, Vaccination an Embankment.

"Great epidemics are like huge tidal waves, which roll
" over any ordinary embankments. It must be borne in
" mind that these embankments are never wholly con-

" tinuous, for the Unvaccinated are like holes in them,
" through which the flood of disease finds its way.   Vac-
" cination is, under ordinary conditions, a sufficient pro-
" tection, but in the presence of a great epidemic it is
" overtopped, and Smallpox spreads over a country,
" attacking the Unvaccinated and those whose protection
" has worn out by age.   As it increases in volume, the
" Vaccinated too are carried away by it; but Vaccination
" is their life-belt, and they rarely perish."

Before discussing this passage, we would draw special
attention to its final affirmation, namely—

"THE VACCINATED RARELY PERISH."

A statement at such open and insolent variance with
fact was never perhaps uttered in the House of
Commons, nor deliberately reproduced in print.   As to
contradict it might seem to make questionable what is
beyond question, we are satisfied to throw it into relief
as evidence of the speaker's audacity.

We said Sir Lyon Playfair was expert at begging the
question : he is equally expert at misleading analogies.
He likened the wilful perils of Vaccination to the risks
of anæsthetics, narcotics, and drinking water: here we
have Smallpox compared to a flood and Vaccination to
an embankment.   What analogy is there between Smallpox and a flood, and Vaccination and an embankment?
A flood overwhelms from without, but Smallpox is begotten in the bodies of the sufferers, and not even then
as an extra affliction, but in substitution for cognate
varieties of disease.   As Mr. John Simon observes—

" Except where there is a definite predisposition, the contagion of Smallpox or Measles has no more power to influence the unpredisposed body
than yeast has power to ferment alcohol or to turn pure water into beer.
. . . For the production of Smallpox there must therefore be a specific
internal as well as a specific external condition."

Consequently it is absurd to speak of Smallpox as if it were an inruption of water or fiery flying serpents. What predisposes to Smallpox? We answer, insanitary conditions of life—the same conditions which generate other forms of zymotic disease. "But why," it may be asked, "does Smallpox at irregular intervals prevail and supersede other forms of fever?" and we reply, We do not know; but wherever we go deeply and widely enough we find Nature equal underneath superficial variance; and Smallpox, we may be sure, is no exception to the common law. Vaccinators, on the other hand, ascribe predisposition to inattention to their rite, and try to prove their case by asserting the greater liability of the Unvaccinated, overlooking the fact that at this day the Unvaccinated are almost exclusively the poor and miserable, involved in the conditions which we maintain predispose to Smallpox. As to Smallpox attacking those whose Vaccination has worn out by age, it is a mere whimsey. Adults in healthy circumstances rarely contract Smallpox, even when epidemic, unless when they induce the disease by Revaccination.

XV.—THE SANITARY REVOLUTION IN SCOTLAND.

"When an epidemic like that of 1870-73 strikes a " population, they become terrified, and they rush in " crowds to be Vaccinated. In 1871 the Compulsory " Law had only existed for eight years in Scotland, and " only the infant population had come under its influ- " ence. But still the people of Scotland, not being cursed " with Anti-Vaccination Societies, rapidly extended Vac- " cination among themselves, and stamped out the

" epidemic. Since then Smallpox has scarcely existed
" in that country. For the last few years the total num-
" ber of deaths have not exceeded 10 per annum."

In order to apprehend the unscrupulous character of
this passage, it is necessary to revert to Sir Lyon Playfair's proclamation in the House of Commons in 1870.
These were his words—

" There cannot be the slightest doubt that Compulsory Laws properly
applied are perfectly equal to stamp out Smallpox as in Scotland and Ireland."

First observe, any reference to Ireland is now dropped;
and the reason is obvious. The Irish facts do not square
with the doctrine advanced. Yet Ireland is Vaccinated
up to the mark of Scotland.

Compulsory Vaccination in 1870 had stamped out
Smallpox in Scotland; but now we are led to infer that
was a mistake. Smallpox had declined to insignificance,
but as the compulsory law had been in force for no more
than eight years, "*only* the infant population had come
under its influence"—as if Vaccination in Scotland had
been initiated in 1863! Then we learn that, moved by
the terror of the epidemic of 1871-73, the Scots rushed
in crowds to the doctors, and "rapidly extended Vaccination among themselves, and stamped out the
epidemic"! We put it to any Scotsman whether this
statement is not fictitious, with scarcely a trace of reality.
Was there any terror?—was there any rush for Vaccination? As for stamping out the epidemic, it passed away
of itself after the manner of all epidemics.

Let us, however, come to figures. The population of
Scotland in 1871 was 3,360,018, and in the epidemic of
1871-73 there died of Smallpox 5,034, representing, say,
25,000 cases in the course of three years; and we are

asked to believe that a population of upwards of three
millions was thrown into a panic on account of the substitution of Smallpox for other forms of illness and death
—a substitution not only circumscribed as to number,
but limited to certain localities, and to certain classes in
those localities! Thousands and thousands of Scots
never knew of the existence of the epidemic outside the
newspapers, nor suffered any alarm on account of it, nor
had any cause for alarm.

Sir Lyon Playfair admits that in 1870 "the infant
population had come under the influence of Vaccination"; and, as we have seen, he avers "*the Vaccinated
rarely perish of Smallpox.*" From the Scots Registrar-
General's Returns we extract the following—

DEATHS BY SMALLPOX IN SCOTLAND OF CHILDREN UNDER
ONE YEAR OF AGE IN 1871-73.

Year.	Vaccinated.	Unvaccinated.
1871	64	142
1872	314	64
1873	139	39
Total—517		245

It can hardly be alleged that in the instance of these
517 babes their "protection had worn out by age," or
that, constituting a tenth of the victims of the epidemic,
their deaths were "rarities."

Scotland used to be a land of Smallpox, for which the
condition and habits of the people were sufficient to
account. Perhaps no form of zymotic disease is so
closely associated with poverty, insufficient and improper
food, and crowded and unwholesome habitations, as
Smallpox; and when we are asked to account for the
diminution of the disease, and the disappearance of
pock-marked faces, surely we are justified in referring to

the vast improvement effected in the condition of the
people during the past forty years! Many young Scots-
men who write in newspapers, and lecture, and preach,
appear to have little or no conception of the hardships
and privations with which their fathers and forefathers
were familiar, or ever realise what was the noisome
atmosphere of houses in cities like Edinburgh and Glasgow before the introduction of water and sewers; or
what would be their horror and terror if the former order
of things were restored. Nowhere has the sanitary
revolution gone deeper, or wrought more vital change
than in Scotland. The worst quarters of the chief
centres of population in Glasgow, Edinburgh, and
Dundee, have been swept out of existence within the
past twenty years; and this contemporaneously with a
marked advance in the personal comfort and refinement
of the people. Sir William Chambers, of Edinburgh, in
his *Story of a Long Life*, published in 1882, observes—

"The first idea that occurs to me is the prodigious change that has taken
place in the social condition of the country. I feel as if living in a new
world. Old notions and prejudices have silently passed away. The denser
forms of ignorance have perished. When I was young all imported food
was taxed. Salt was taxed to more than thirty times its natural value;
soap was taxed; leather was taxed; candles were taxed; window-lights
were taxed. At one time, as I recollect, tea was sold at 8s. a pound, and
sugar was four times the price it is now. Through the removal of so many
exactions, and from other causes, *the humbler classes are now better paid for
their labour, better fed, better clothed, and better housed.*"

Granting these prodigious changes, as granted they
must be, why should we attribute to a whimsical cause
like Vaccination what is so reasonably accounted for by
the profound and extensive modification of the conditions in which Smallpox is fostered? The very means
which a sanitarian would prescribe for the reduction and
extirpation of Smallpox have been brought into force,

and yet we are asked to believe that all these changes
count for nothing, and that the decline of Smallpox in
Scotland is due to Vaccination, and to nothing but
Vaccination !

XVI.—SANITATION AND SMALLPOX.

" These great reductions in Smallpox Mortality are, I
" believe, wholly due to Vaccination; but my Hon. Friend,
" the member for Leicester, attributes them to improved
" Sanitation and to the improved habits of the people.
" But if that were true, this Sanitation must equally
" affect other diseases besides Smallpox, and no doubt
" it does, but to what amount ? If we compare the
" period of Gratuitous Vaccination [1841-53] with that
" of efficient Compulsory Vaccination [1854-81], the
" Registrar-General tells us that, among children under
" five, Smallpox Mortality has decreased by 80 per cent.,
" while that from all other diseases has only decreased
" by 6 per cent. As age advances beyond fifteen years
" Mortality does decrease in other diseases, probably
" from Sanitation, but it increases as regards Smallpox,
" showing how little influence that has as a factor in
" governing the progress of that disease. The cause of
" the increased mortality in Smallpox at advanced ages
" is probably that there are still many Unvaccinated,
" and that among the Vaccinated the protective power
" wears out as age advances. The fact, however, con-
" clusively shows that improved Sanitation has little
" connection with the large reductions in the rate of
" mortality from Smallpox over the whole community."

First, a few words as to the changed incidence of
Smallpox with respect to age.

Whereas Smallpox used to be almost exclusively a
disease of the young, it has latterly been leaving the

young, and becoming commoner among adults; and we
are asked to believe that this change is due to the protection afforded by Vaccination to the young and to the
exhaustion of the protection in adults. As to this explanation, we have to observe, that the changed incidence
has been progressive, and that the young were as fully
vaccinated in 1860 as in 1880; and if so, how can Vaccination account for the progressive movement? It is
all very well for the Registrar-General to assume that
the increased stringency of the law represents increase
of Vaccination, but when we refer to the statistics of
Vaccination they fail to bear out the assumption. In
this connection we recall an observation of Dr. A. Wood
before the Committee of 1871 ; he said—

> " There is a tendency in the human mind, and especially in the edu-
> cated human mind, to assign a material cause for everything, and therefore
> Vaccination is often unjustly seized upon as the material cause of some of
> those things." No. 4467.

It is thus with the progressive change in the incidence
of Smallpox. An explanation is wanted, and Vaccination is seized upon, especially as the explanation is
supposed to make for the glory of the rite and for its
repetition. "The uneducated human mind" *will* have
explanations, but as to innumerable phenomena the wise
recognise they have no explanation, and confess their
ignorance until a verifiable explanation is forthcoming.
Diseases are always undergoing permutation, and why
and wherefore it is hard to make out. Who will tell us
why Smallpox fell off toward the close of last century,
and through the earlier portion of the present. Why,
for instance, the deaths from the disease in Vienna
dropped from an average of 835 annually between 1791
and 1800 to 27 in 1803 and 2 in 1804, whilst, neverthe-

less, the total mortality of the city remained unaffected. Why, again, Scarlet Fever, once regarded as a trivial ailment, is now described as "the most dreadful scourge in Europe."

Sir Lyon Playfair says that where Smallpox has fallen off, the reduction is *wholly* due to Vaccination, and therefore *not at all* to Sanitation. It is an extraordinary opinion, explicable, perhaps, in those who trade in Vaccination and thrive by it, but repeated by one who either respects himself, or knows enough to qualify him for speech on the subject—what shall we say? Sanitation without influence on Smallpox! Smallpox a form of zymotic disease amenable in all forms to Sanitation—except in the one form of Smallpox! It is difficult to argue the matter seriously, but that an absurdity, however gross, should be credible and mischievous, is warrant sufficient to condescend to it.

Lord Shaftesbury stated no more than what seems to us certain and notorious when he said in the House of Lords in 1853—

"It is perfectly true that Smallpox is chiefly confined to the lowest classes of the people, and I believe that with improved lodging houses the disease might be all but exterminated."

If it is objected that Lord Shaftesbury is not a medical man, or that opinion may have shifted since 1853, why, then, we have the same evidence in different terms from Dr. Alfred Carpenter, who, speaking at Brighton in 1881, thus delivered himself—

"The class of disease called Zymotic includes Smallpox, Fevers, Cholera, Diphtheria, *et id genus omne*. The places in which such diseases will be most fatal are pretty well known. The conditions producing fatality are of man's making, and can be removed by the action of man. What are those conditions? In a few words, they are due to those changes which result from the act of living. The natural products of secretion, or the excreta which are either retained too long within the body itself, or, being excreted, are not passed on to the vegetable kingdom for utilisation and re-application to man's wants—these excreta are the mainsprings of this class of disease, when allowed to remain where they ought not to be. *It would be as impossible for Zymotic Diseases to exist among us as it is for fish to live long out of water, if all excreta were rapidly removed and immediately utilised.* The presence of Zymotic Disease in our midst is evidence that some kind of excreta is retained somewhere in too close proximity to particular individuals."

Nothing can be more explicit, nothing more consonant with scientific experience. Dr. Carpenter refers the existence of Smallpox and its kindred to the tolerance of filth and stench ; holding that apart from filth and stench it would be as impossible for them to exist as live fish out of water. He, moreover, adduced Her Majesty's convict prisons as evidence of the truth of his contention, that it is possible to live securely exempt from zymotic disease. In those select and exclusive establishments, inhabited by men and women drawn from the most un-healthy classes, the death-rate is no more than about 8 per 1000; and this marvellously low mortality is ascribed by Dr. Carpenter to the observance of those sanitary conditions whereby Smallpox and its kindred are made impossible. Among the triumphs of the science of health, nothing has been more satisfactory than the demonstration that zymotic diseases hang together, and that together they may be deprived of existence. The commercial spirit, however, is as pronounced in Medicine as in Manchester, and in order to find room for the vaccinator's rite, and to perpetuate the gains annexed thereto, it has been contrived to separate Smallpox from its kindred, to deny that it is preventible by similar means, and to proclaim that for it there is but one preventive—namely, the preventive revealed by the immortal Jenner! Such an inversion of the logic of science, not to mention common-sense, might well be

deemed incredible, had we not the word of Sir Lyon
Playfair before us, endorsed by the ignorance of the
House of Commons. The absurdity of the position is
reduced to childish apprehension by Dr. Garth Wilkinson's Catechism—

Q. When Whooping-Cough is not rife, what is that due to?
A. Nature.
Q. When Scarlatina is not rife, what is that due to?
A. Nature.
Q. When Cholera is not rife, what is that due to?
A. Nature.
Q. When Smallpox is not rife, what is that due to?
A. Vaccination.
Q. When other diseases in the course of time have become mild or died
out, what is that due to?
A. Nature.
Q. And when Smallpox has become mild or died out, what is that due to?
A. Vaccination.

Further, Sir Lyon Playfair argues that if Sanitation
had reduced Smallpox it must have equally reduced other
diseases, but that no such reduction is apparent. But is
no such reduction apparent? It is, of course, absurd to
compare Smallpox with *all* other causes of death, for as
Dr. Collins observes, "to compare Smallpox with all
diseases other than Smallpox is to compare things
totally incomparable." When, however, we take Smallpox with its kindred Fevers, we sometimes find there is
a marked parity in their decline, and, sometimes, as it
were, a substitution of one for the other—much Fever and
little Smallpox, and much Smallpox and little Fever.
Following Sir Lyon Playfair's erratic arrangement of
periods, but omitting 1847-49 for which the figures for
Fever are not given, the Registrar-General reports—

DEATHS PER MILLION LIVING.

Years.			From Smallpox.			From Fevers.
1850-53	...	...	310	...	...	986
1854-71	...	...	223	...	...	940
1872-80	...	...	156	...	...	473

The like concomitant decline of Fever and Smallpox was noted by Dr. Farr at the close of last century, when as yet Vaccination was unknown, and at the beginning of this century, when to Vaccination was wrongfully ascribed the credit.   Dr. Farr says—

"Fever progressively declined from 1771, and in nearly the same proportion as Smallpox.   Thus—

DEATHS PER 10,000 LIVING.

		1771-80	1801-10	1831-35
Fever,	...	621	264	111
Smallpox,	...	502	204	83 "

Here is another view of the case.   Smallpox has not fallen off, as it ought to have fallen off, and Dr. Cameron and others assert that the disease is kept alive and diffused by the extensive use of Smallpox Cowpox (that is, Smallpox inoculated on the cow) for Vaccination, and they have reason and figures to justify their suspicion. The Registrar-General in his Report for 1880, says—

"The decennium which closed with the year 1880 was one of lower mortality in London than any of the preceding decennial periods. . . . These facts are strong evidence that the sanitary efforts of recent years have not been unfruitful. . . . The evidence in support of this position is rendered still stronger, if, instead of fixing our attention upon the total mortality, we take into consideration its causes.   For it will be found that the saving of life was almost entirely due to diminished mortality from causes whose destructive activity is especially amenable to sanitary interference—namely, the so-called Zymotic Diseases. . . The death-rate from Fever fell nearly 50 per cent. . . That of Scarlatina and Diphtheria fell 33 per cent. . . *One disease alone in this class showed exceptionally a rise, and no inconsiderable one.   This was Smallpox, which owing to two great outbreaks of 1871-72 and 1877-78, gave a death-rate nearly 50 per cent. above its previous average.*"

Here we have the Registrar-General confessing to a low rate of mortality from zymotic disease coincidently with a high rate from Smallpox ; and if, at the end of the current decennium the incidence is reversed and he has to report a low rate from Smallpox and a high rate from other forms of zymotic disease, how shall we define the advantage?

The development of Smallpox Mortality is thus tabulated by the Registrar-General—a startling and instructive array of figures—

	Deaths from Smallpox.		Death-rate from Smallpox per 100,000.	
	England.	London.	England.	London.
1841-42, 47-50, 6 years,	29,522	8,416	29	40
1851-60, ...	42,071	7,150	22	28
1861-70, ...	34,786	8,347	16	28
1871-80, ...	57,422	15,539	24	46

In presence of this development of Smallpox, we have to bear in mind the injury to health inflicted by the universal practice of Vaccination, coupled with its great and useless expense. At the Conference on Animal Vaccination in 1879, Dr. Ballard argued that if it were not for the interference of such epidemics as 1871, the records of Vaccination would be perfectly satisfactory: whereon Mr. Enoch Robinson observed, that Dr. Ballard reminded him of a bankrupt who avowed that he would be perfectly solvent if it were not for his confounded losses.

What is Sanitation? Essentially it is the action of oxygen, the free play of the atmosphere around the processes of life. In so far as air is excluded and hindered in its operation, insanitary conditions are developed wherein zymotic disease has place and scope. Rural habits and modes of existence may be as faulty as urban, but they are less deadly than when aggregated in centres of population where the wholesome air is less copiously present. Of this we have an illustration in Seaton's *Handbook of Vaccination.* The Scots Registrar-General having recorded in his annual reports the Smallpox Mortality, 1st, in the islands of Scotland; 2nd, in the rural districts including villages and towns of the mainland ; and, 3rd, in towns of 10,000 inhabitants and upwards, Dr. Seaton classified the returns for ten years, as in the following table—

| YEARS. | Smallpox Deaths per 100,000 Living. | | |
	In the Islands.	In Rural Districts and Small Towns.	In Towns of 10,000 Inhabitants and upwards.
1855	17	34	75
1856	11	26	84
1857	16	11	61
1858	6	8	17
1859	5	10	46
1860	21	33	83
1861	4	16	44
1862	1	6	27
1863	10	37	87
1864	19	48	78
Totals, ...	110	229	602

"There is no reason for supposing," adds Dr. Seaton, "that the insular and rural districts of Scotland are better vaccinated than the large towns: *the probability is that it is just the reverse.* Their small relative mortality from Smallpox is due to their being much less exposed to the infection." Just so ; but is it not the purpose of Vaccination to neutralise infection ? Therein Vaccination fails, whilst more abundant air, which stands for involuntary Sanitation proves highly effectual. Q. E. D.

XVII.—IMPUTATION AND ACCUSATION.

"The results which I have described are the figures of "the Registrar-General, and are derived from an exami-

" nation of long periods, so as to include the epidemic
" and non-epidemic years. How is it that they sound
" so differently from the figures given by the mover of
" of the resolution? He startles you with large figures,
" such as 40,000 deaths in the Metropolis during an
" epidemic, and he rarely throws them into comparable
" rates of mortality. He also relies chiefly on the returns
" of London mortality, and puts on one side the saving
" of life throughout the country. But I intend to meet
" him on his own ground, and to show that the case for
" Compulsory Vaccination is best supported by epidemic
" periods."

The preceding paragraph is a characteristic exhibition
of Sir Lyon Playfair's controversial method—he describes
his own practice, imputes it to his adversary, and con-
demns it. The movement is artful, and effective—until
detected. There is nothing which impresses hearers and
readers of Mr. Taylor more than his unreserved production and discussion of evidence; and it is to this candour
and scientific impartiality that he owes his success in
opening the "closed" Vaccination Question. To charge
him, therefore, with the tactics of the venal crew who set
themselves "to preserve Vaccination from reproach" at
any cost, and manipulate statistics at discretion, may
pass for clever, but it is a sort of cleverness that leaves
a bad savour when the first effect is exhausted. When,
let us ask, did Mr. Taylor startle the House of Commons
with a 40,000 metropolitan epidemic? Is it that Sir
Lyon Playfair, having the House in hand, prejudiced
and ignorant, took them as capable of any incredibility?
With an access of assurance, he further accused Mr.
Taylor of "relying chiefly on the returns of London
mortality," as if (were the accusation true) there could
be any harm in testing the value of Vaccination in a

population vaccinated to the extent of 95 per cent. But why, why should Sir Lyon Playfair complain of reference to London? Would he have us forget that his annual Smallpox Mortality of 3,000 per million over the whole country prior to Vaccination is derived from a conjectural London death-rate unwarrantably extended to the United Kingdom? Strike that magical statistic from his grasp, and the presumptuous little conjurer would be left gasping on his back. But he is going to perform another feat—to show us that "Compulsory Vaccination is best supported by epidemic periods;" that is to say, by outbreaks of Smallpox among Vaccinated and Revaccinated people! *Hey, presto!*

———

XVIII.—Smallpox in the Franco-German War.

"Just as 'Black Death' followed in the train of the "Wars of the Red and White Roses, so did malignant "Smallpox follow the camps of the French and German "armies in 1870. Both Powers had about half a million "of men in the field, but under very different conditions. "Germany was quite prepared for the war, and had its "troops under perfect organisation. All its recruits "were Revaccinated. In ordinary times France also "encourages the Revaccination of the recruits, and in the "year before the war about 40,000 recruits were so "treated. But Prussia does it more systematically, and "in the same year Vaccinated 216,426 of its soldiers."

This statement is loose in detail, but the intention is obvious, being that the German soldiers were thoroughly and the French indifferently Vaccinated. The answer is, that the French army was completely Vaccinated. In the words of Dr. Bayard, writing in 1872, "Revaccination originated in France. Every young soldier is revaccinated on his entrance into a regiment. Our army knows of no exceptions." As to Vaccination therefore the conditions of the armies were equal.

Smallpox, it is said, "*followed* the camps of the French and Germans in 1870." Is the observation intended for science or for fancy? What is meant by Smallpox *following* a camp? Smallpox is apt to originate in filthy camps, and to escape the pest it frequently suffices to move elsewhere. It is said, too, that it was *malignant* Smallpox which *followed* the camps. But is there any such entity as Malignant Smallpox? Whether Smallpox be mild or malignant is, as John Hunter taught, dependent on the condition of the sufferer. The crop takes its character from the soil. Smallpox that is mild in a child may be malignant in a drunkard.

"Nevertheless, the Paris garrison in the early part of "1870 had scarcely any Smallpox, while 1,000 of the "civil population had already died."

That was before the war broke out. What was surprising in the immunity of the Paris garrison? Smallpox is chiefly a disease of the young, badly fed, and badly housed amid foul odours. That soldiers in the prime of manhood, exercised in the open air, and lodged in barracks built and arranged to ensure health, should escape Smallpox, even when Smallpox was rife, we should take as matter of course.

The scene is changed. The French army, defeated in the field, was led captive to Germany. Then said Sir Lyon—

"The recruits who were hurried in from the provinces "soon added to the military deaths. Dr. Leon Colin, the

5

" Physician-General of the French army, has published
" a work on the Smallpox epidemic during the war.   He
" tells us that the levies hurriedly raised were unvac-
" cinated.   [*Nay, not unvaccinated; but not revaccinated.*]
" I give his own words—

'The different armies raised thus in haste, and placed in the field without time for Revaccination, were exposed both at their places of gathering
and in their marches to the attack of this epidemic '—

" And the consequence was that during 1870 and 1871
" no less than 23,469 died of the disease, of whom 1,600
" died in the garrison of Paris, out of an army of 170,000.
" The Smallpox followed the German camps also, but
" only 263 of their well-revaccinated soldiers died.   I
" contend that the German soldiers escaped on account
" of their revaccination.   Many hundreds of them were
" prisoners in Paris during the siege, and only one of
" them was attacked by a mild form of Smallpox.   Could
" a more pronounced experiment on a large scale have
" been made in regard to the value of Vaccination?"

Before dealing with the 23,469 French soldiers alleged
to have died of Smallpox, we would say a word concerning the citation of Dr. Colin as authority for the statement.   When Mr. P. A. Taylor discredited the statistic
in the House of Commons, Sir Lyon holding up Colin's
book, *La Variole*, said—

" I got it from the Physician-General of the French
" army."

The summary answer to which is, that he did not.   The
statistic is neither in Colin's book, nor is Colin in any
way responsible for it.   This, Sir Lyon was subsequently
compelled to admit.   Colin, therefore, being an impossible authority, Sir Lyon had to look out for another,
and in the authorised edition of his speech these words
are interpolated—

" I give these figures on the authority of the report of
" Dr. Thilenius to the German Reichstag, and of similar
" figures given at the meeting of the Statistical Congress
" in St. Petersburg."

What have we here? German authority for a French
statistic! Why, a reference to Dr. W. B. Carpenter would
be as much to the purpose as to Dr. Thilenius! The
second reference to the Statistical Congress at St. Petersburg conducts us however to the original authority,
namely, a stray newspaper paragraph! Here it is—

"THE RESULTS OF REVACCINATION.—According to a statement made
at the Statistical Congress held this year in St. Petersburg, the total number of deaths from Smallpox in the German army during the recent Franco-
German war was 263. This small mortality is attributed to the system of
Compulsory Vaccination which every man who enters the army must undergo. On the other hand, in the French army, where Vaccination is not
Compulsory, the number of deaths, as stated by a French authority, was
23,469. This terrible difference (says the *Wiener Medizinische Wochen-
schrift*) must puzzle the greatest opponents of Vaccination."

This appeared in the *British Medical Journal* in 1872,
and was reprinted in the *Anti-Vaccinator* of Nov. 1, 1872,
with various instructive comments. It was shown that
the French army was completely revaccinated; and if,
it was argued, notwithstanding, 23,469 fell victims to
Smallpox, no more conclusive proof could be desired of
the uselessness of Vaccination and Revaccination.

Vaccinists have used this 23,469 to an endless extent
for the past ten years, and yet not one of them has taken
pains to inquire whether the anonymous statement in an
Austrian medical journal was true! We cannot trace
the statistic prior to its appearance in the Austrian journal, which might be varied thus—

One day at St. Petersburg in 1872 somebody said that
France lost 23,469 soldiers by Smallpox in 1870-71 because they were not revaccinated.

But we can go further.   Dr. W. B. Carpenter trafficked largely in the astounding statistics ; and, according to his habit, serenely confident that what he wishes true *is* true, he incontinently pledged himself to Mr. Wheeler to substantiate the figures or withdraw them.   It was a rash vow.   Earl Granville was appealed to, and the resources of the Foreign Office brought into requisition. In vain !   The French authorities had to admit that the number of deaths from Smallpox in the war of 1870-71 was unknown.   The confusion was too great for systematic registry.   Dr. Carpenter was therefore driven to retractation, which painful ceremony he accomplished in a letter to the *Daily News* of August 7, saying—

"If I have erred in adopting, without sufficient authority, a statement which had every appearance of being trustworthy, my opponents should remember that they, too, are fallible."

Apparently trustworthy !   Why, it was fabulous on its face !   Bearing in mind that, even in the worst circumstances, there is some proportion between cases of Smallpox and deaths from Smallpox, let us ask ourselves what number of cases 23,469 deaths would stand for ? Colin states that in the French army of 170,000 besieged in Paris, 1870-71, there were 11,500 cases of Smallpox and 1,600 deaths.   At the same rate, 23,469 deaths would represent 166,000 cases, and an army of 2,400,000 men ! What more need be said ?

The statement was fabulous on its face, but such is the credulity of the advocates of Vaccination that it is difficult to overtax it ; and if Sir Lyon Playfair and Dr. W. B. Carpenter have shown themselves no more critical than a couple of old women, they may allege in their excuse that they are no worse than the majority of the

House of Commons, the newspapers, and the public, who shrieked with delight over the " crushing demonstration" from the Franco-German war, now confessed to have been bogus! Unfortunately Dr. Carpenter's retractation goes but a little way to correct the widely diffused error. Every newspaper gave publicity to the false statistic, and editors expatiated on its " crushing" effect; yet, with a few exceptions, no publicity has been given to the correction. It is discouraging; and yet why should we be discouraged? A cause that is thus defended, whatever its triumph for the moment, is bound to go down; and it will carry not a few reputations with it.

Of course, we are not concerned to deny that the French suffered more severely from Smallpox than the Germans. So much was to be expected. The influence of the mind on disease ought never to be forgotten. In Holmes's *System of Surgery*, vol. i. p. 174, we read—

"Extreme mental depression has also been thought to predispose to the occurrence of Pyœmia. In the Franco-German war Pyœmia was more prevalent in the French than in the German Hospitals. The want of morale and despondency was much commented on by M. Gosselin, and he is described as having taken the greatest trouble to raise the confidence of his men, believing strongly that their condition of extreme mental depression from want of success much predisposed them to the occurrence of Pyœmia."

Had the French rolled back the German host on Berlin, crushed and demoralised, with the sick and wounded huddled into hospital under any shelter, the incidence of Smallpox would have been reversed, whether the Germans had been Vaccinated, Unvaccinated, or Revaccinated. And yet, perhaps, not altogether reversed; for the Germans had mastered the first principles of military hygiene, and no great war was ever conducted with fewer fatalities from sickness than on the German side. It was far otherwise with the French, and those whose lot it was to minister to their sufferings have appalling stories to relate, and well-nigh incredible, of ignorance, mismanagement, and neglect.   In Busch's *Bismarck in the Franco-German War*, 1870-71, we read—

> "Count Maltzahn had been to Fort Issy. Heaps of filth and an abominable smell. 'Had they no latrines?' 'Apparently not.' 'They are an uncleanly people,' said Bismarck, reminding us of the horrible arrangements in the town school-house at Clermont, and the similar state of things at Donchery."

The French were put upon the defensive, crowded together, and besieged, whilst the Germans were in the open, marching, and with choice of camps. Dr. Colin remarks—

> "Virulent diseases, especially the eruptive fevers, are more especially developed by troops in garrison; and, on the contrary, they become mild or disappear by life in the free air and in camps."

Hence he tells us, that when the Gardes Mobiles were suffering from Smallpox in 1870, he recommended that they should leave their barracks and go into tents so as to have the full benefit of fresh air.

Where, then, is the force of Sir Lyon's question—

"Could a more pronounced experiment on a large "scale have been made than in this Franco-German "war?"

The asserted conditions of the experiment are proved untrue, whilst the real conditions would account for little Smallpox on one side, and much Smallpox on the other, irrespective of Vaccination.   Nevertheless, such was the hurry and confusion of the titanic conflict that we question whether it is known how many German soldiers perished of Smallpox in 1870-71. The figures 261 and

263 cited by Sir Lyon Playfair were given as 3,162 by Herr Steiger, Swiss Minister of the Interior, at Berne on 6th February, 1883. Methodical and exhaustive statistics of the causes of death are not easily kept in a great war ; and the more neatly they are tabulated, the graver reason there is to suspect fiction.

It is a trifle, but characteristic of his reckless turn : Sir Lyon Playfair said, " Black Death followed in the train of the Wars of the Roses"—an anachronism of a century. Black Death had made its broad mark on English history in 1348. It was the Sweating Sickness that accompanied Richmond's continental mercenaries in 1435.

XIX.—BERLIN AND THE GERMAN ARMY.

" It was not because they were Germans that Small-
" pox spared the German army ; for it attacked the city
" of Berlin in January, 1871, and was nearly as fatal to
" the civil population there as it was in Paris during the
" siege. I contend that the German soldiers escaped on
" account of their Revaccination."

Such as it is, this argument implies that the citizens of Berlin were Unvaccinated. But were they Unvaccinated ? On the contrary, no urban population in Europe was more completely Vaccinated ; and when deaths from Smallpox happened to be few, credit was claimed for the law which made Vaccination compulsory, and a certificate of the rite an indispensable preliminary of education, of public employment, and of marriage. Yet in Vaccinated Berlin 5216 died of Smallpox in 1871,

and 1198 in 1872! In Prussia at large, equally Vaccinated, the Smallpox deaths, which in 1870 were 4,200,
rose in 1871 to 69,839, equivalent to a death-rate of
2,430 per million, or very nearly twice and a half the
Smallpox death-rate in England for the same year.
Could there be a more conclusive demonstration of the
inutility of Vaccination?

But it may be urged, that whilst the army suffered
slightly from Smallpox the inhabitants of Berlin suffered
severely.   True; but soldiers and citizens were alike
Vaccinated; and for the difference between them we
must look elsewhere.   The soldiers were in the field and
the citizens were cooped together.   But the difference
was still wider.   The army consisted of men in the prime
and vigour of life, who had passed the age when sus-
ceptibility to Smallpox is greatest.   To compare an
army in the field with a city a third of whose population
is in the condition of childhood, is to stand convicted of
absurdity that would be incredible in any question other
than that of Vaccination.   Last century, ere Vaccination
was heard of, Smallpox among adults was about as uncommon as Scarlatina and Measles in the same class at
this day; and whilst it still remains true that Smallpox
is chiefly an affection of the young, yet, since Vaccination, and especially Revaccination, have come into vogue,
the disease exhibits an increasing tendency to attack a
higher range of ages.   That it should be so is what
might be expected, a variolous habit of blood being so
diligently cultivated.   To illustrate what is meant, let us
set before us two tables—one of a severe epidemic of
Smallpox in Berlin in 1746, and the other of the
epidemic of 1871.

SMALLPOX WITHOUT VACCINATION.

Age-Classes.	Berlin, 1746.		
	Persons Living.	No. of Deaths.	Deaths per 1000.
0—1 year	2,000	41	20·5
1—5 ,,	6,560	129	19·5
5—10 ,,	7,120	15	2·1
10—20 ,,	13,360	1	0·1
above 20	50,960	0	0
	80,000	186	2·3

SMALLPOX WITH VACCINATION.

Age-Class.	Berlin, 1871.		
	Persons Living.	Deaths.	Deaths per 1000.
0—1 year	18,917	1,038	54·6
1—5 ,,	69,176	1,189	17·2
5—10 ,,	71,011	243	3·4
10—20 ,,	144,422	172	1·2
above 20	519,043	2.443	5·7
	822,569	5,085	6·2

Let any who are interested in statistics consider these
tables, and point out the advantage derived from Vaccination. In the first place, the rate of mortality from
Smallpox in Vaccinated Berlin in 1871 was threefold
that of Unvaccinated Berlin in 1746; and whilst in 1746
not a single adult died of Smallpox, 2,443 perished in
1871, constituting nearly half of the total mortality!
Such is the fruit of Vaccination and Revaccination!
There is nothing peculiar about these tables, or about
Berlin. The facts they exhibit are common facts that
are found repeated everywhere.

XX.—Leipzig and Leicester.

" The Hon. Member for Leicester bases his argument
" on the fact that the town which he represents, though
" so badly vaccinated, has had little Smallpox, or prac-
" tically none at all in recent years.　That is equally
" true of well vaccinated and badly vaccinated towns
" throughout the country.　In 1872 Leicester was not a
" badly vaccinated town, and perhaps my Hon. Friend
" might argue that was the reason why it had 313
" deaths.　Well, I earnestly hope it may not soon come
" under an epidemic wave, for I can give him an
" instance of a large town which did neglect Vaccination
" among its people, and of the results which followed
" when an epidemic struck it.　Leipzig was the centre
" of a most zealous propaganda against Vaccination, in
" which the Anti-Vaccination associations were power-
" fully assisted by the Press.　The result of their
" agitation was that infantile Vaccination had been
" greatly neglected, and Leipzig was in that happy state
" which Leicester now rejoices in, of having refused to
" vaccinate its children.　Leipzig had been singularly
" free from Smallpox, as Leicester now is.　In 18 years,
" from 1851 to 1870, it had only 29 deaths from this
" disease, and the Anti-Vaccination propaganda pointed
" to it with triumph.　But the pandemic reached this
" town of 107,000 inhabitants toward the close of 1870,
" and killed 1,027 of its people, or at the rate of 9,600
" per million.　The infantile death-rate was terrific.
" There were 23,892 children living under fifteen years
" of age, and among them were 715 deaths—actually 3
" per cent., or at the terrible rate of 30,000 per million.
" I have given an example and a warning, but I doubt
" whether the Hon. Member for Leicester will profit by
" it.　If the Hon. Member for Leicester cares to know
" my authority for these statements, I refer him to the
" accounts of the Leipzig epidemic by the German phy-
" sicians, Wunderlich and Thomas."

Here was judgment and warning! Leipzig despising Vaccination, Smallpox fell upon the inhabitants thereof, and slew 1,027, of whom 715 were hapless children! But whoever said or supposed that to refrain from Vaccination was to be secure from Smallpox? And if Vaccination was despised by certain scoffers, was it neglected? And did Smallpox select and slay the Un-vaccinated? On the contrary, the Vaccinated constituted an overwhelming majority of the sufferers. Of 1,611 in one hospital, only 29 were Unvaccinated; and of 1,727 in another, only 139 were in like case. Of 117 children received in the General Hospital all were found Vaccinated. The reader will naturally exclaim, "How, then, could Sir Lyon Playfair commit himself to a statement so extraordinary, detection and exposure being certain!" It is for the romancer to explain. At anyrate, Leicester is not likely to be terrified into Vaccination by the Leipzig bogey, conjured out of a few figures and an unscrupulous fancy.

XXI.—THE BRITISH ARMY IN 1871-72.

"This epidemic became pandemic, for it not only "devastated Europe, but invaded both North and South "America, as well as the South Sea Islands. Before "describing its ravages in this country, I may as well "say how far it influenced our 90,000 revaccinated sol- "diers. It entered our Army, as it did this country, in "1871, and lingered in it during 1872, but during those "two years it only killed 42 soldiers. The epidemic of "1871, however, struck the civil population of England "and Wales strongly, and was exceptionally severe in "the metropolis."

The epidemic of 1871-72 *only killed* 42 soldiers—men in the prime and vigour of life, quartered in barracks where skill is exhausted in preserving the human animal in health ; and we are invited to believe that they escaped lightly. Had they escaped completely there would have been little reason for surprise. Anti-Vaccinists agree with Lord Shaftesbury that " Smallpox might be all but exterminated with improved lodging-houses"; and lo ! they are confronted with a partial exemplification of their own doctrine !

In 1871-72 there were 344 cases of Smallpox and 42 deaths in the Army, all revaccinated—a curious commentary on the infallible prescription which saves even nurses in Smallpox Hospitals. Let us also observe that of the 42,000 who died in the 1871-72 epidemic throughout England and Wales, 26,000 were under 20 years of age, representing a marked diminution of risk in the adult population ; and that if we take the 42,000 deaths to represent, say, 250,000 cases, there remained the not inconsiderable multitude of 22,750,000 who entirely escaped ; in that respect being more fortunate than the revaccinated British Army of 90,000.

XXII.—2,000, 3,000, 4,000, AND 5,000 PER MILLION.

" I mentioned that, before Vaccination was introduced,
" in last century the deaths from Smallpox throughout
" the country were 3,000 per million over periods em-
" bracing epidemic and non-epidemic years, but in the
" heavy malignant epidemic of 1871-2 the death-rate
" was 928 per million over the whole country. The
" average death-rate from Smallpox in the metropolis

" before Vaccination was 4,000 per million, and in the
" great epidemic year, 1871, it was 2,420 per million.
" So that even in this exceptionally severe epidemic the
" death-rate was only about one-half of that of average
" years in last century."

If iteration could convert uncertainty to certainty and
error into truth, Sir Lyon Playfair might pass for a
successful practitioner. Here we have once more Lettsom's conjectural London Smallpox Mortality of 3,000
per million converted into National Smallpox Mortality
with the fiction circumstantial that it embraced " epidemic and non-epidemic years." As possibly the iteration of truth may be as effective as that of its reverse, let
us repeat that the National Smallpox Mortality of last
century is unknown, and that it is an imposture to pretend otherwise. Even that of London is unknown,
apart from the bills of mortality, and these are untrustworthy. " The areas from which they were drawn," says
Dr. W. A. Guy, " were frequently changed, and there
are sundry omissions of places and classes of people ";
and as London enlarged its borders a more and more
numerous population escaped from the record. Lettsom
guessed that 3,000 a year died of Smallpox in London,
taking the population at a million, and *assumed* that a
similar rate for the United Kingdom would give 36,000
a year. The National Health Society circulates tracts in
which this estimated 36,000 is boldly transformed to
40,000 per annum! The variety on this point, not to
use a rougher epithet, is startling. In the reports of the
National Vaccine Establishment for 1811 and 1818, the
London mortality of the last century is stated as 2,000
annually: in the reports of 1826 and 1834 the number is

raised to 4,000 : and in those of 1836 and 1839 it is given as 5,000 !   Thus Sir Lyon Playfair has not been singular in the exercise of his fancy.   Possibly if we knew all, we should find him astonished at his own moderation.

___

XXIII.—VACCINATED AND UNVACCINATED LONDONERS.

" The Anti-Vaccinators say, Why did it enter into a
" metropolis of which at least 95 per cent. of the people
" are Vaccinated?   But that 5 per cent. means a residue
" of 190,000 Unvaccinated persons, besides all the im-
" perfectly Vaccinated, and those in whom the protective
" effects have worn away by age.   Surely that is soil
" enough for a good harvest of Smallpox. . . . The
" Anti-Vaccinators point to the fact that there were
" absolutely more cases of Smallpox among the Vaccin-
" ated than among the Unvaccinated during the epi-
" demic—a fact which obviously must arise when 95 per
" cent. are Vaccinated."

Obviously !   Why obviously?   The understanding upon which Vaccination was received from Jenner and paid for by the English people, ran thus—

"In abundant instances it has been uniformly found that the human frame, when once it has felt the influence of the genuine Cowpox, is never afterwards, at any period of its existence, assailable by the Smallpox."

Nor can it be said that Jenner retreated from his position.   He remained firm in his persuasion after an experience of five-and-twenty years, writing a few days before his death in 1823—

"My opinion of Vaccination is precisely as it was when I first promulgated the discovery.   It is not in the least strengthened by any event that has happened : it is not in the least weakened."

This assurance has, however, vanished; and now when it is objected that the majority of the sufferers from Smallpox are Vaccinated, the fact is admitted as *obvious*, inasmuch as 95 per cent. of the population have undergone the Jennerian rite, warranted in primitive times to ensure an indefeasible salvation !

It is said that in the Unvaccinated 5 per cent. there is "surely soil enough for a good harvest of Smallpox"; but what evidence is there ontside the wishes of Vaccintors (proved under an illusion from the outset) that the Unvaccinated provide the soil? In Germany, where such facts are more methodically and impartially registered than in England, it has been found that when Smallpox breaks out, it is among the Vaccinated, and that not until the epidemic is established are the Unvaccinated attacked. So much might have been predicted. In so far as Vaccination sets up a variolous habit of blood, it must predispose to Smallpox.

Again, it is said that the Vaccinated whose protection has worn away by age contribute to the soil for a good harvest of Smallpox ; but that also is no more than a convenient assumption. The majority of those who suffered from Smallpox in 1871-72 were young and were Vaccinated ; and what a contemptible pretence it therefore is to say of Vaccinated adults overtaken by the disease, "Their protection must have worn out !"—said, too, of Vaccinated parents suffering in common with their recently Vaccinated children !

The "wearing out" of the protection of Vaccination is a supplement to the mitigation excuse. It was first claimed that to be Vaccinated was to be secure from Smallpox for life. Then under stress of disaster, it was

said that although Vaccination might not prevent Smallpox it made it milder—milder even in death! Then
the "wearing out" excuse was invented, but Jenner
would never hear of it; and in the report of the National
Vaccine Establishment for 1819 it was thus neatly
refuted—

"It appears to us to be fairly established, that the disposition in the
Vaccinated to be affected by Smallpox *does not depend upon the time that
has elapsed after Vaccination;* since some persons have been so affected
who have been recently Vaccinated, whilst others who have been Vaccinated 18 or 20 years have been inoculated with Smallpox and exposed to its
contagion with impunity."

And in the report of the same Establishment for 1851
we read—

"It may be expedient to remind the public of *the established fact,* which
the Board upon former occasions anxiously insisted upon, that the restriction of the protective power of Vaccination *to any age, or to any term of
years,* is an hypothesis contradicted by experience, and wholly unsupported
by analogy."

But notwithstanding "the established fact," and the
contradiction of experience and analogy, the "wearing
out" excuse was too useful to be dispensed with. It
not only assisted in preserving Vaccination from reproach, but it served to justify the new and lucrative
practice of Revaccination. Consequently the excuse
prevailed, and by Sir Lyon Playfair is set forth as un-
questioned matter-of-fact. When on one side there is
an interest to have something believed, and on the
other an inclination to believe, what is incredible!

That 95 per cent. of Londoners are or ever were Vaccinated, we take leave to doubt. Until recently, 80 per
cent. Vaccinated was the utmost that could be shown
out of the entire births, and allowing for the dead
Unvaccinated, and for the dead Vaccinated, the total
of 95 per cent. alive Vaccinated is got at by a process

highly conjectural. The fact may be that 10 per cent. are Unvaccinated.

There is no occasion to dispute that Smallpox is commoner among Unvaccinated than among Vaccinated Londoners, unless as to the degree of frequency, concerning which we are not only ignorant, but as to which the testimony of Vaccinators is untrustworthy. The Unvaccinated in London consist mainly of the houseless, the miserable, the outcast—people whose environment predisposes to Smallpox, and contributes to the worst results when Smallpox occurs. Anti-Vaccinists have a doctrine to which they appeal, and by which it is fair they should be judged. By that doctrine it is taught that Smallpox is associated with unwholesome conditions of life, which conditions are those of Unvaccinated Londoners. It is further maintained, that in so far as the like conditions are those of Vaccinated Londoners, they are as liable to Smallpox as the Unvaccinated, if not more liable. They insist that if these conditions are taken into consideration they account for the phenomena of the disease—Vaccination being irrelevant. If therefore it were proved that a much larger proportion of Unvaccinated than of Vaccinated Londoners were afflicted with Smallpox it would simply confirm the doctrine of the Anti-Vaccinists, just as the comparative exemption of the Army confirms the same doctrine in the other way.

———

XXIV.—Who are the Unvaccinated?

"Looking at the epidemic generally throughout the " kingdom, the argument may be put in this way.

6

" When the 1871 epidemic went over the country, there
" was an infant population of more than three millions
" under 5 years of age. It consisted of Two Classes in
" daily intercourse with each other ; but one Class (the
" Vaccinated) was thirty or forty times more numerous
" than the other. They, however, lived intermixed,
" residing in like houses, eating the same food, and
" breathing the same epidemic air. In the Class which
" was thirty or forty times the size of the other, 413
" deaths occurred, while in the smaller Class 1,780
" deaths occurred—that is, four deaths occurred in the
" smaller Class for every death which occurred in the
" Class which was thirty or forty times larger. If you
" convert that into a rate of mortality for each Class, you
" will find that the rate of mortality was from 120 to
" 160 times greater among the Unvaccinated than among
" the Vaccinated children. The only circumstance which
" differentiated these millions of children was Vacci-
" nation, and as the incidence of Smallpox was so
" enormously different in its mortality according as the
" Class was or was not Vaccinated, the conclusion as
" to a very large amount of protection in the case of
" children is irresistible. If you carry the argument
" to the general population of all ages, the Registrar-
" General tells us that in the same number of people
" the Vaccinated give 1 death, and the Unvaccinated
" 44 deaths."

In the Smallpox epidemic of 1871 there died 23,126
in England and Wales, of whom 7,770, or one-third of
the whole, were children under 5 years of age. What
proportion of these were Vaccinated and Unvaccinated
is unknown with any approach to precision. Sir Lyon
Playfair says 413 were Vaccinated (who by the way,
" rarely perish "!) and 1,780 were Unvaccinated ; a total
of 2,193 which leaves 5,577 unaccounted for. Obviously
Sir Lyon has a poor head for figures, but as his inten-

tion is plain, we may disregard his arithmetic, and close at once with what is essential, namely, his assertion that the mortality from Smallpox among Unvaccinated children in 1871 was 120 to 160 times greater than among Vaccinated, and that Vaccination was the cause of the difference.

Firstly, we question the authenticity of the figures adduced for comparison. As to the relative numbers of the Vaccinated and Unvaccinated, there is great uncertainty. Dr. Buchanan, the head of the Medical Department of the Local Government Board, in a Memorandum concerning a year of London Smallpox, 1880-81, in which 1,532 died, gave 321 as Vaccinated (who "rarely perish"!) 637 as Unvaccinated, and no fewer than 507 *whose condition as to Vaccination was Unknown*—this, too, in London, where facts of such moment might surely be ascertained if there were any disposition to ascertain them. We cite the instance from Dr. Buchanan to show how wide is the margin for conjecture in stating in exhaustive terms the numerical relation of the Unvaccinated to the Vaccinated.

Secondly, we hold that the registration of deaths from Smallpox as Unvaccinated is subject to unqualified suspicion. Over and over again has it been proved that the Vaccinated dead are registered as Unvaccinated. Death is taken as evidence of the absence of Vaccination. It is often argued with all the assurance of simplicity, "If the child had been Vaccinated, the child could not have died;" or, should the fact of Vaccination be indisputable, then it is said, "The Vaccination must have been defective to be thus good for nothing." In many of these cases, Vaccination is either not stated in the certificate of death, or "Unvaccinated" is boldly filled in.

In writing thus we make allowance for invincible prejudice, and for the conviction that those who question the efficacy of Vaccination, or still more discourage its practice, are enemies of the human race, whom it may not be unlawful to treat after the manner described by Lord Wolseley in his *Soldier's Pocket-Book*—

"As a nation we are bred up to feel it a disgrace to succeed by falsehood. We will keep hammering along with the conviction that 'honesty is the best policy,' and that truth always wins in the long run. These pretty sentences do well for a child's copy-book, but the man who acts upon them in war had better sheathe his sword for ever."

It is natural that subjects of this persuasion should be indisposed to recognise the failures of Vaccination, should endeavour to conceal them, and should snatch at any excuse to sustain the prestige of the practice and deprive scoffers of any opportunity of triumph. Of this tendency, blind and not yet blind, Sir Lyon Playfair is a flagrant example. He involves himself in contradictions and inconsistencies—relates as it were unconsciously the deaths of hundreds and thousands of the Vaccinated from Smallpox, and then wheels round and avers that "the Vaccinated rarely perish"!

"The only circumstance," he says, "which differentiated the millions of children in the epidemic of 1871 was Vaccination"—an observation repeated from Dr. Buchanan in his Memorandum on London Smallpox, where it is thus given—

"As no one suggests that the Vaccinated and Unvaccinated classes live under conditions differing from each other in their influence on Smallpox, *unless it be this one condition of Vaccination*, it follows that the Vaccinated are much less liable to die of Smallpox than the Unvaccinated."

Such an observation is nothing short of astounding.

That the Vaccinated and Unvaccinated differ only in the one condition of Vaccination is a statement so wildly untrue that only a man ignorant of his fellow creatures, or contemptuous of their intelligence, could venture to make. Who are the Unvaccinated? They are, first, children too feeble to endure Vaccination, and therefore liable to perish under any prevalent malady; and, second, the offspring of the vagrant and wretched classes, who, being without fixed domicile, have escaped the vigilance of Vaccination spies and informers. No difference in the Vaccinated and Unvaccinated save in the one condition of Vaccination! It would be difficult to conceive an assertion with any air of plausibility at such explicit variance with fact.

If Vaccination *versus* Non-Vaccination is to be tried, let the conditions be equal. Do not pit Unvaccinated feebleness and wretchedness against Vaccinated vigour and well-being. Compare the children of Vaccinists with those of Anti-Vaccinists in Keighley, Dewsbury, or Leicester, class with class, state of life with state of life; nor shall *we* shrink from the issue. On the other hand, if in a public hospital the Vaccinated and Unvaccinated were discriminated in cases of Pneumonia and Scarlatina, we have little doubt that a lower death-rate would be recorded among the Vaccinated, inasmuch as the Unvaccinated waifs and strays who drift into hospital are broken-down outcasts. But would it therefore be fair to argue that Vaccination was as good against Pneumonia and Scarlatina as against Smallpox?

Absurd as is Dr. Buchanan's statement, it is aggravated by Sir Lyon Playfair. He says of the Vaccinated and the Unvaccinated, that they "*lived intermingled, residing in like houses, eating the same food, and breathing the same epidemic air"!* In the Birkenhead Smallpox epidemic of 1877, Mr. Francis Vacher drew attention to "the especial prevalence of the disease among young persons," and that of 603 persons affected, "an overwhelming majority were derived from the families of labourers and artizans," there being indeed only 6 exceptions from the middle classes. There was nothing peculiar in this respect about Birkenhead, and we only cite it as an ordinary and average instance. Even in last century it was notorious that Smallpox was chiefly prevalent and deadly among the poor and wretched. Cross in his description of the Norwich Epidemic of 1819, states that its victims were "confined almost exclusively to the very lowest of the people;" and what was true of Norwich in 1819 continues true at this day. People have Smallpox because they live or lapse into the conditions of Smallpox—not because they are Unvaccinated; and to represent the subjects of the disease as living intermixed, without other distinction than the absence of Vaccination Marks, is an additional note of that reckless disregard of reality which characterises Sir Lyon Playfair's advocacy.

XXV.—Smallpox Past and Present.

"The Vaccination Acts are not sufficient to resist a "great epidemic wave, but they act as a breakwater and "lessen its force. In the last metropolitan epidemic of "1881 it was found that 90 in every million of the "Vaccinated died from its effect, but no less than 3,350 "per million of the Unvaccinated perished. The reason

" for this is that even when malignant Smallpox strikes
" the Vaccinated, it becomes modified or mild in 73 per
" cent. of the cases, and it retains its virulent form in only
" 27 per cent. But when it strikes the Unvaccinated,
" 97½ per cent. of the cases pass through the virulent
" form, and only 2½ per cent. become mild. Hence the
" perils of attack are vastly greater among Unvaccinated
" than among the Vaccinated."

Several points in this citation invite remark. For
example, the Epidemic Wave and the Breakwater—
analogies which correspond to nothing in Smallpox or
Vaccination. Likewise the assertion, that "even when
Malignant Smallpox strikes the Vaccinated, it becomes
modified or mild in 73 per cent. of the cases, and mild
only in 2½ per cent. of the Unvaccinated"—an assertion
which is like a deliverance from the Grand Academy of
Lagado. Smallpox is known for malignant when it is
malignant, and no otherwise : there would be just as
much sense in describing a showery day as a modified
or mild wet one—modified or made mild by some incan-
tation. Moreover, in his definition of the varieties of
Smallpox, Sir Lyon Playfair said—

"Thirdly, comes the Black or Malignant form of Smallpox, which rarely
attacks the Vaccinated, but when it does it proves as fatal to them as to
the Unvaccinated ; for 95 per cent. of the persons attacked by this form of
Smallpox die."

But now we are informed, that it becomes mild in 73 per
cent. of the Vaccinated and in 2½ per cent. of the Unvaccinated !

These, however, are trivialities, but interesting as
additional illustrations of the license of advocacy. Our
business is to deal with the main position—the asserted
greater mortality of Smallpox among the Unvaccinated.

Broadly and firmly we meet this assertion with contradiction. It is untrue. We do not care to enter into details of percentages, of less in one city and more in another, of less at one time and more at another—with such details we are provided in bewildering profusion. Our ground is good, and there we abide immoveable. Smallpox, according to all valid testimony, is much the same disease that it ever was, and when, therefore, we are asked to believe that the Unvaccinated at this day, *because* Unvaccinated, die at twice or thrice the rate of the Unvaccinated a hundred years ago, why then we are apt to express ourselves after the manner of honest men when confronted with such imposture as presupposes their imbecility.

We have seen (p. 24) that Tissot gave the mortality of epidemic Smallpox last century as about 13 per cent., or 1 death out of 8 attacked. Dr. Seaton, in his *Handbook of Vaccination*, observes—

"Dr. Jurin, writing early in last century, laid it down as the result of his investigation, that of persons of all ages taken ill of natural Smallpox, there will die 1 in 5 or 6."

Jurin included in this estimate hospital Smallpox, nearly always more fatal than Smallpox treated at home. Among patients out of infancy and in good circumstances, the mortality was much less. Thus, Isaac Massey, apothecary of Christ's Hospital, London, writing in 1723, gave his experience of Smallpox among the lads of that institution—

"There are generally near 600 children in the nurseries at Ware and Hertford, constantly filling the places of the boys who go off from London. It hath sometimes happened that great numbers have been down of the Smallpox, and 'tis but seldom that the House is free, or not long so; yet. I dare say, and Sir Hans Sloane, I presume, will say so too, that in twenty years there have not died above 5 or 6 of the distemper, and in the last nine years there died but 1.

"As I have said, we have lost but 1 Smallpox patient these nine years, although 1,800 children have been in the House during that time; and I declare to have met with no unequal success in other families among children about the same ages (that is between 8 and 15) where I have been concerned; and I doubt not but many of the Learned Faculty, as well as some others of my profession, can say as much from their own experience and observation."

In the great epidemic of 1752 in Boston, Massachusetts, when one-third of the inhabitants were attacked and 539 died, the mortality did not exceed 10 per cent. Including infants, always the most likely to succumb, it was a common reckoning that of 6 or 7 who had Smallpox, 1 died. Coming to the present century, after the introduction of Vaccination, we have the evidence of the Epidemiological Society in 1852, collected from 156 medical practitioners in various parts of England, that the Unvaccinated died at the rate of 19·7 per cent., or as nearly as possible 1 in 5—the Unvaccinated being then chiefly limited to the poor, who suffer most severely from whatever disease.

With these facts before us, showing that when all were Unvaccinated the death-rate was under 20 per cent., we are now told everywhere that the Unvaccinated die at rates varying from 40 to 60 per cent., whilst the death-rate of the Vaccinated undergoes correspondent declension. That people should entertain, and repeat, and asseverate such statements proves their ignorance of the very elements of the case whereon they presume to dogmatise.

XXVI.—Vaccinated and Unvacinated in Hospital.

"An analysis of 10,000 cases in the metropolitan "hospitals shows that 45 per cent. of the Unvaccinated

" patients died, and only 15 per cent. of Vaccinated
" patients. . . . These statistics of disease correspond in
" countries which have compulsory laws and in those
" which have not. Across the Atlantic there is no
" direct, though much indirect, compulsion, and no mo-
" tive to falsify statistics of mortality. But in America
" the mortality among the Unvaccinated was even
" greater than in London during the pandemic. In Bos-
" ton, the rate of mortality among the Unvaccinated was
" 50 per cent.; in Philadelphia, 64 per cent.; and in
" Montreal, 54 per cent.: while the deaths of Vaccinated
" patients ranged between 15 and 17 per cent."

Dr. W. B. Carpenter declines to read the *Vaccination
Inquirer*, the Editor having, he says, stated—

"That a Table which I had constructed of Smallpox Mortality, from
data supplied to me by the medical officer of the Homerton Smallpox
Hospital, *was not to be believed, even if sworn to.*"

The Editor's words we find to have been as follows—

"We print the Homerton Return at Dr. Carpenter's request, desiring
that he should establish his position to his complete satisfaction. It is
hardly necessary for us to repeat once more the single word, Incredible !
We know the mortality from Smallpox in Pre-Vaccination times; it was
about 18 per cent., or the same in the total of cases as at the present day.
When, therefore, we are told that the Unvaccinated die at Homerton at
the rate of 44 per cent., we laugh the communication to scorn. It is in
vain to multiply figures in proof. We say they are incorrect; that we
know they are incorrect; and that, however sworn to, we should still
reject them as incorrect. In this matter we are hardened and hopeless
unbelievers."

This is strong language, but in so far as the strength
is that of truth, it need not offend us. The argument
is clear. The rate of Smallpox Mortality when all were
Unvaccinated is known ; and if it is asserted that the
Unvaccinated at this day die at double or treble the
rate of last century, what resource has a rational man
other than incredulity? When, moreover, we have the
total cases of any present day hospital, and find the

mortality identical with that of last century, what other conclusion is possible than that the discrimination of the patients into Vaccinated and Unvaccinated, showing a low death rate for the one and a high death rate for the other, must be erroneous? It was a pity that Dr. W. B. Carpenter, instead of taking offence, did not set himself to explain the difficulty, if he knew of any explanation.

Attempts are continually made to confound Anti-Vaccinists with private and partial evidence. Smallpox, they are told, broke out in a certain household: the Vaccinated escaped or recovered, whilst the Unvaccinated died. The household experience is sometimes magnified to that of a village or city; and the obvious conclusion is enforced with superfluous emphasis.

Stories of this kind are always to be received with reserve or disbelief. They usually proceed from those who have a pecuniary or professional interest in Vaccination, and we know that if facts told against the practice, they would be suppressed in order that the Jennerian rite might be "preserved from reproach." Wherever it has been possible to scrutinise evidence in favour of Vaccination, it has either turned out false, or has been susceptible of a different interpretation. There was Leeds, for instance, where a strong case for Vaccination was made out, but which Mr. Pickering in *The Statistics of the Leeds Smallpox Hospital Exposed and Refuted*, proved to be a tissue of fiction. The detection and exposure of the imposture was attended with much labour and difficulty, and but for Mr. Pickering's intervention, it would have passed without question for veracious. It is much easier to concoct fables than to explode them, and fabulists reckon on the difficulty for impunity.

When the moralist is confronted with instances of successful immorality, he says they must be illusory, for to righteousness alone belongs permanent success. When the man of science is confronted with what appears irregular or exceptional in Nature, he falls back on universal law. He recognises the order of the world, and confiding in that order, he says, if the fact be a fact, it is in some way misunderstood, and when we know more, we shall find it included in the harmonious whole. And thus we treat the asserted successes of Vaccination. It is in vain to tell any one who understands the laws of health that such a disease as Smallpox can be arrested or mitigated by a device like that of Jenner's. Coincidences may favour Vaccination, as coincidences favour all forms of quackery, but it is a first caution in logic to distinguish *post hoc* from *propter hoc.*

To make the question of Hospital Smallpox plain, we subjoin two tables, the first showing the mortality last century, when all were Unvaccinated, and the second the mortality this century, when the majority of the patients were Vaccinated and the minority Unvaccinated.

I.—BEFORE VACCINATION.

Year.	Authority.	Cases.	Deaths.	Deaths Per Cent.
1722	Dr. Jurin quoted by Dr. Duvillard,....................	18,066	2,986	16·53
1746-63	London Smallpox Hospital,	6,456	1,634	25·30
1763	Lambert quoted by Dr. Duvillard,....................	72	15	20·8
1779	Rees' Cyclopædia,............	400	72	18·0
		24,994	4,707	18·83

II.—AFTER VACCINATION.

Year.	Authority.	Cases.	Vac-cinated.	Deaths.	Deaths Per Cent.
1836-51	Mr. Marson's Hospital Report, ...	5,652	3,094	1,129	19·97
1870-72	Metropolitan Hospitals,...	14,808	11,174	2,764	18·66
1876	Do. Do.	1,470	—	338	23·0
1871-77	Homerton Hospital (Dr. Gayton),..................	5,479	4.236	1,065	19·43
1876-80	Dublin Hospital (Dr. Grimshaw),..............	2,404	1,956	523	21·7
1876-80	Metropolitan (Jebb), ...	15,171	11,412	2,677	17·6
1881	Deptford (M'Combie), ...	3,185	2,654	552	17·3
		48,169	34,526	9,048	18·78

These Tables convey two important lessons. First, they show that before the introduction of Vaccination the percentage of deaths from Smallpox was no higher than at present. And, inasmuch as the deaths in the second Table include a large majority of Vaccinated, demonstration is afforded that Vaccination has had no effect in diminishing mortality. Second, that Smallpox as treated at the present day, and Smallpox as treated by the medical men of the 18th century, is the same *unmodified* disease, exacting the same ratio of victims to cases.

Our contention is, that conditions being equal, Vaccination makes no difference, unless to the disadvantage of the Vaccinated. Still it may be asked, How is it that men, who cannot be charged with conscious misrepresentation, vouch for an extraordinary excess in the mortality of the Unvaccinated? We answer, inasmuch as the Unvaccinated died last century at much the same rate as the Vaccinated and Unvaccinated in this, it is for those who vouch for the novel development of mortality to account for the contradiction they sustain from statistics. Nevertheless we may offer some explanation.

The root of the error, we apprehend, is to be found in the classification of cases under a blinding prepossession in favour of Vaccination. It is taken for granted that a severe case of Smallpox is necessarily an Unvaccinated case ; and as in such cases the Vaccination marks are usually invisible, they are unhesitatingly registered as Unvaccinated. We do not say that such classification is always fraudulent in intent : on the contrary it is often honest with the honesty of inbred faith and fanaticism. Mr. Vacher, in his account of the Birkenhead epidemic, says they did not mind what a patient said, or what his friends said of his Vaccination. They looked at his arms, and if they saw Vaccination marks, he was entered as Vaccinated, and if they saw no vaccination marks, he was entered as Unvaccinated. Under this formula, it is plain the worst cases of Smallpox must pass for Unvaccinated with a corresponding result in the death rate. In the Glasgow epidemic of 1871-72 a similar rule prevailed, and in Dr Russell's report there is the following confession—

"Sometimes persons were said to be Vaccinated, but no marks could be seen, very frequently because of the abundance of the eruption. In some cases of those which recovered, an inspection before dismission discovered Vaccine Marks sometimes 'very good.'"

Thus the Unvaccinated recovered and were found Vaccinated. How many of the same order died and passed beyond correction, who can tell? And yet it is to statistics thus collected that we are required to bestow confidence and to admit that evidence is against us !

There are no doubt differences in the character of

admissions to hospitals in this century and last. Such is the terror of Smallpox at the present day, that children, and even infants, are hurried into hospital ; and especially the offspring of the homeless, in whom are the majority of the Unvaccinated. The fatality of Smallpox among the young is not recognised as it ought to be. Dr. Vernon of Southport in his excellent lecture, *Why Little Children die*, observes—

" It is remarkable how much more numerous the deaths from Smallpox are during the first year of life than in any subsequent year. Not only so, but nearly as many deaths from this terrible disease occur during the firs' year as during the next four, and one-eighth of all the deaths from Small-pox occur during the first year. I do not suppose there are so very many more cases of the disease, but the fact is they nearly all die. I never saw a child under one year of age recover from Smallpox."

Moreover, as we have pointed out, the Unvaccinated are as a class the most miserable of the people, who in any epidemic would exhibit the heaviest death-rate. If, therefore, it were proved from the hospitals that they died at a greater rate than the Vaccinated, there would be no reason to resort to Vaccination for the explanation of the difference.

It is much to be regretted that the question can be so inadequately discussed, but we have to remember that such evidence as we possess is largely derived from Vaccinators who disclose nothing to the disadvantage of their craft, unless inadvertently. They profess unlimited allegiance to truth—if not adverse to Vaccination. Like the company of clergy who met to consider the ecclesiastical situation, and to take whatever steps conscience might dictate—except out of the Church of England, they are willing that everything should be known— except anything to the discredit of Vaccination.

Dr. William Munk, physician of the Highgate Small-

pox Hospital, London, gave some interesting evidence
before the Smallpox and Fever Hospitals Commission
in 1882.   The Highgate Hospital is supported by
voluntary contributions, accommodates 100 patients,
and accepting payment from some of them, includes a
higher grade than the general and pauper institutions.
Among much that does not immediately concern us,
Dr. Munk testified—

"Smallpox is becoming in each epidemic a more severe and fatal disease.
If you take the epidemics of the present century, each successive epidemic
has become more severe and the mortality far greater.   The percentage of
Vaccinated cases at Highgate is now 94.   In 1826 it was 38 per cent.   In
1838 it had become 40 per cent., and has gone on increasing until in 1879
it was 94·6 per cent.   In latter years the mortality has been as follows—

1877—19 per cent.	1880—12·4 per cent.
1878—15·2 ,,	1881—13·8 ,,
1879—13·25 ,,	

In face of such a statement may we not ask, Wherein
is the profit of Vaccination?   The ratio of Vaccinated
patients is in excess of the Vaccinated population, and
the mortality is that of last century when all were
Unvaccinated.

Sir Lyon Playfair says the mortality of the Unvaccinated in America was even greater than in London:
"it was 50 per cent. in Boston, 64 per cent. in Philadelphia, and 54 per cent. in Montreal."   Of course it
was: we are bound to be outnumbered in America in
Smallpox as in most other things.   Medical men there
are more numerous than with us, more needy, and
hard-set for a living, and they advertise themselves with
corresponding assiduity: Dr. Martin and his miracles
being a fair exemplification of the style prevalent and
respectable.   Animal Vaccination is widely practised,
and there are factories for the production of Cowpox,
which is sold wholesale, retail, and for exportation with

all the arts of quackery. Our English Vaccinators are
not over scrupulous, but we lack words to describe the
conjoint ignorance and impudence of the American
variety. If Jenner proved anything it was that Cowpox
was no defence against Smallpox ; and because it was
no defence, he set it aside and prescribed Horsegrease
Cowpox obtained from the inoculation of Horsegrease,
or more correctly Horsepox, on the cow. Latterly he
used and diffused Horsepox neat as "the true and
genuine life-preserving fluid." Yet Martin and others
drive a roaring trade in Cowpox with the credulous mob
under the sign of the immortal Jenner! Medical men
in this country are generally inclined to agree with Dr.
Ballard "that scientific observation and reasoning give
no countenance to the belief that Smallpox ever will be
eradicated ;" but Dr. Austin Flint of New York is of a
different mind. In the *North American Review* for
June, 1881, he says—

"Smallpox may be blotted out of the list of existing diseases by extending to the whole human race the security afforded by Vaccination and
Revaccinations made everywhere compulsory. If they who resist their
enforcement were alone the victims of the disease, society could afford to
let them die 'as the fool dieth.' The question is whether society shall
suffer on account of their folly. The right of society to protect itself in
this matter is as clear as that of placing under restraint a homicidal maniac."

The homicidal maniac we take to be Dr. Austin Flint
himself. The compulsory Vaccination and Revaccinations of the whole human race is a project worthy of a
compatriot of Mr. Jefferson Brick, and the means advocated remind us how a republican in name may be the
worst of tyrants in fact.

"The deaths of Vaccinated patients in America,"
continues Sir Lyon Playfair, "ranged between 15 and
17 per cent. during the pandemic." But in the Boston

7

epidemic of 1752, when all were Unvaccinated, the mortality was no more than 10 per cent.! Sir Lyon has, however, to account for a more startling discrepancy, for he has told us "that Vaccination is the life-belt of the Vaccinated, and they rarely perish"; but nevertheless from 15 to 17 per cent. of Vaccinated Americans perished, notwithstanding their life-belt.

———

XXVII.—GAIN FROM VACCINATION.

" The Hon. Member for Leicester treats these hospital
" statistics as wholly incredible, but they are verified by
" the hospital statistics in our provinces, and also by those
" of other countries during the pandemic. He can only
" deny them by assuming that a huge conspiracy exists
" among the medical men of all nations for the purpose
" of injuring mankind at large. A conspiracy has some
" supposed advantage to be gained by its success. But
" how can doctors all over the world benefit by keeping
" doctors poor through making their patients healthy?"

The reader will observe that Sir Lyon Playfair is never so ingenuous and audacious as when his case is most hazardous—the art whereby attention is diverted from weakness. The hospital statistics in which he has been dealing can only be denied, he says, "by assuming a huge conspiracy among the medical men of all nations." Medical men of all nations, forsooth! Why, we defy a medical man of any nation to stand forward and prove a death-rate of 40 or 50 or 60 per cent. among the Unvaccinated, in or out of hospital, *because* Unvaccinated. A huge conspiracy! O dear, no! It would be as ab-

surd to describe Witchcraft as a conspiracy. Vaccination
is a delusion as Witchcraft was a delusion, and the
manner of people who were carried away with the one,
and the evidence thought conclusive, exhibit singular
affinities with those of the other   To a large extent the
faith in Witchcraft was as disinterested as the faith in
Vaccination, but to a certain extent it was associated
with private ends, and dishonest; whilst none were more
virulent than the latter toward any signs of mercy or
scepticism, or more voluble in the expression of orthodox
reprobation—all which manifestations of baser human
nature Anti-Vaccinists see reproduced within their own
experience, and understand.   They recognise that with
many Vaccination is honestly believed, but with others
is complicated with professional pride, and associated
with gain present and with gain prospective.   Trained
in the persuasion that Smallpox is a measureless affliction from which Vaccination is the sole deliverance, they
consider it allowable, and even commendable, to conceal
its failures and disasters from the vulgar, and when
necessary to prevaricate in its favour.   The public are
dealt with as outside the franchise of science—as children
or invalids who are entitled to no more than it is good
for them to know.   In a little book, *Notes from Sick
Rooms*, 1883, by Mrs. Leslie Stephen, written with much
good sense, we read—

"If trouble should come, and it is important that the invalid should be
kept in ignorance, her watchers must make peace with their consciences as
best they can ; and if questions are asked, they must 'lie freely.'"

Here we have the esoteric and exoteric positions
revealed.   On the one hand are the vaccine experts, and
on the other the ignorant multitude, whom for their own

good it is expedient to hold faithful to Jenner; and
when therefore there is occasion, it is excusable to "lie
freely."

"A conspiracy," observes Sir Lyon, "has some supposed advantage to be gained by its success;" and then
with an artless turn inquires, "How can doctors all over
the world benefit by keeping doctors poor through
making their patients healthy?" How, indeed! That
the Vaccine Fever should, unlike any other Fever, make
or leave its subjects healthy, is sufficiently extraordinary;
but that the doctors who generate the said Fever should
be kept poor thereby, and yet be so madly intent, as
they show themselves, in extending the impoverishing
practice, is still more extraordinary. Sir Lyon, we fear,
is as maladroit in human nature as in arithmetic.
Whatever misery Vaccination may beget, it stands for
anything but loss to its practitioners.

For example, few have any notion of the sum annually
spent in this country upon the Vaccination of the Poor.
In the Twelfth Annual Report of the Local Government
Board, we find the following statement—

PUBLIC VACCINATION.—ENGLAND AND WALES.

	1881.	1882.
Vaccination Fees and Expenses............	£87,745	£97,196
Awards for superior Vaccination............	16,903	14,264
	£104,648	£111,460
Number of Vaccinations....................	533,005	516,340

There is much that is instructive in these figures. We
often hear of gratuitous Vaccination, but there is no
such thing. As to Vaccination we are Socialists. There
used to be persons and societies who vaccinated gratui-
tously, but their work has been long superseded. If the

poor pay nothing for the Vaccination of their children, it is because they are paid for out of the pockets of those who pay rates and taxes. The Vaccination of 516,000 poor men's children at an average cost of 4s. 6d. each is a handsome poll-tax for which no conceivable outbreak of Smallpox could furnish an equivalent. Vaccination pays better, steadily and perennially, than Smallpox— Smallpox, we mean, in conjecture, for Smallpox with Vaccination remains.

When we remember that the songs to the glory of Vaccination are sung by the recipients of this immense sum of money and their professional associates, it is easy to understand their fervour and persistency; and it is rather hard that we should be so frequently taken to task for our imputation of bias on the part of these mercenaries. We ask any one with the least pretence to acquaintance with human nature (historic or contemporary) whether any iniquity, however flagrant, thus endowed would not be fought for with tooth, and nail, and craft? It would be outside reason and experience to expect otherwise. It is well to be charitable, but surely charity does not imply imbecility!

To the poll-tax of 4s. 6d. on the children of the poor, with yet further gains from the illnesses consequent on Vaccination, there have to be added the more liberal fees obtained from the wealthier classes who do not send their babes to the Vaccination Station, but have them operated on at home. Likewise the gains from the Revaccination of soldiers, sailors, policemen, postmen, and the entire civil service. What money is picked up for Revaccination is seen in the case of our public schools. The doctor and the masters affect to be

alarmed about some real or rumoured case of Smallpox
in the neighbourhood, and as a precaution all the boys
are revaccinated, and 10s. 6d. entered against each in
his bill.   It is but fair to add that when some hundreds
of pounds are thus realised, the doctor does not get all
the money.   He has his share, and the operation is
repeated at a convenient interval.

With these sources of gain, there is little cause for
surprise that medical men uphold Vaccination, recommend compulsory Revaccination, and are furious with
those who impeach the practice.   We do not say that
they defend Vaccination, knowing it to be a delusion,
on account of the lucre attached thereto; but it is
according to all experience of human nature that gain
exercises a constraining influence over judgment, conscience, and conduct; and that no corporate body,
whatever the virtue of individuals included in it, ever
surrendered emolument, however reprehensible, unless
through external compulsion.

We may take it, therefore, for certain, that Vaccination
will have to be disestablished and disendowed in the
teeth of the medical profession.

———

XXVIII.—NON-EFFECT OF SMALLPOX ON TOTAL MORTALITY.

" The arguments of Anti-Vaccinators are so protean
" that one never knows what they are.   When they
" assert that Vaccination is no protection against Small-
" pox, and does not lessen mortality, our reply is
" conclusive.   But in the same breath they admit a

" largely diminished mortality by Vaccination, but say
" that it does not lessen the sum of human mortality,
" for when Smallpox deaths lessen, other diseases
" increase; and they seem to invite us to enter a Golden
" Age when all of us should take Smallpox as of yore in
" order to protect us against other diseases."

We can no more answer for all Anti-Vaccinists than
Sir Lyon Playfair can answer for all Vaccinists; but
that Anti-Vaccinists assert Vaccination is no protection
against Smallpox, and in the same breath admit a
largely diminished mortality by Vaccination is surely
an imputation of stupidity too gross to be credible.

What Anti-Vaccinists maintain, and prove with ease,
is that the presence of Smallpox does not raise, nor the
absence of Smallpox lower the ordinary death-rate.
Addressing the House of Commons in 1878, Sir Thomas
Chambers said—

"You cannot show that Vaccination has reduced deaths, or saved a
single life. There may be no Smallpox, but the disappearance of Smallpox
is by no means equivalent to a reduction of mortality."

M.P.'s were astonished and incredulous; but ignorantly.
The fact is incontestable; and Dr. Robert Watt of
Glasgow had the signal distinction of detecting and
setting it forth in the year 1813.

Glasgow was an established haunt of Smallpox last
century, the disease being accountable for 20 per cent. of
the total mortality; almost exclusively that of children.
Toward the close of the century, a fall in Smallpox set
in, and Vaccination being introduced early in the present
century, and Smallpox continuing to fall off, Vaccination had the credit. By 1812, the Smallpox mortality
had been reduced from 20 per cent. to less than 4 per

cent., and great was the rejoicing. " See, see !" it was exclaimed, " See what Vaccination has done for us !"

Watt was writing a treatise on Whooping-Cough, and in the course of his work had occasion to make a careful examination of the registers of death in Glasgow, and the decline in Smallpox came under his notice. It was most satisfactory. Since, he argued, the mortality from Smallpox has so largely declined, fewer children must have died ; but to Watt's amazement the facts did not answer to the logic. He wrote—

" To ascertain the real amount of this saving of infantile life, I turned up one of the later years, and, by accident, that of 1808, when, to my utter astonishment, I found that still a half, or more than a half, of the children born in Glasgow perished before the tenth year of their age ; I could hardly believe the testimony of my senses, and therefore began to turn up other years, when I found that in all of them the proportion was less than in 1808 ; but still, on taking an average of several years, it amounted to nearly the same thing as at any former period during the last thirty years. This was a discovery I by no means expected, and how it could have come to pass appeared to me inexplicable."

Pursuing his inquiry, Watt discovered that Smallpox as a cause of death had been replaced by other causes, especially by Measles, and though Smallpox had abated, the trade of the undertaker continued undiminished.

Dr. Farr has reviewed Dr. Watt in the 30th Annual Report of the Registrar-General, 1869, and not only confirmed his conclusion, that notwithstanding the partial disappearance of Smallpox from Glasgow "nearly the same number of children died as before of other forms of disease," but he has provided an intelligible explanation of the phenomenon—

" The Glasgow victims were gathered together from all quarters, from the Highlands, from Ireland, and from elsewhere ; they were lodged in conditions unsuitable to human life. . . . To render them unassailable by the matter of Smallpox was not enough, for it left them exposed to the other forms of disease. Thus, in a garden where the flowers are neglected, to keep off thistle-down merely leaves the ground open to the world of surrounding weeds.

"To operate on mortality, protection against every one of the fatal zymotic diseases is required ; *otherwise the suppression of one disease-element opens the way to another.*"

Dr. Farr thus exactly expresses what we wish to enforce. Whether Smallpox prevail or disappear is of little importance. What is of importance is the prevalence of disease and death, and not the presence or absence of any special factor when the total result is constant and the measure of violated physiological laws.

Here is another passage from Dr. Farr, which still further establishes our position—

"Out of 1000 born in Liverpool, 518 children were destroyed in the first ten years of their life, some by Smallpox, many by Measles, Scarlatina, Whooping-Cough, many by Typhus and Enteric Fever ; one disease prevailing in one year. another disease prevailing in another, *but still yielding the like fatal results.* This represents what Dr. Watt found at Glasgow long ago. Out of 1000 children born in London, 351 died under ten years of age by Zymotic Diseases and other causes ; the deaths are less by 167 than the deaths in Liverpool. How much less is the loss of life by these diseases in the healthy districts of England ! There, out of 1000, only 205 children die in the first ten years of life. The enormous difference cannot be ascribed to Vaccination, as common in town as in country ; the protection of life against Smallpox alone leaves it still at the mercy of the dangerous diseases of the insalubrious city."

About our case, then, there need be no doubt, nor need Sir Lyon Playfair affect inability to grasp our arguments. If they are obscure or protean, we refer him to Dr. Farr, and when he has mastered Dr. Farr, he may see more clearly. With regard to Smallpox, we hold that it is of no use trying to contend with it singly ; that it is a member of a group of diseases, which come and go and take each other's places as if they were one and interchangeable ; and that to repress Smallpox effectually, it must be repressed with its associates by the maintenance of the common conditions of health ; by comprehensive sanitary measures ; and beyond all

by the persuasion and practice that health itself is the
best defence of health.

These statements appear like truisms, and yet how
far they are from truisms the ignorance of our adversaries
bears witness. Whenever there is an outbreak of Smallpox the event is discussed as if every life lost was an
extra life lost, when inquiry would reveal that not more,
but probably fewer, are dying than usual. In Prague,
from 1796-1802, the general mortality was 1 in 32, at a
time when the Smallpox mortality was 1 in 396⅔; but
in 1832-55, when the Smallpox mortality was only
1 in 14,741⅓, the general mortality was still 1 in 32⅓.
What Dr. Watt discovered in Glasgow in 1813 will be
found repeated and illustrated wherever we choose to
look. The years distinguished by large Smallpox mortality are by no means years of the largest *general*
mortality. Thus take forty years in London, 1841-80,
and we find these results—

LONDON.

YEARS OF LEAST SMALLPOX.		YEARS OF MOST SMALLPOX.	
Smallpox deaths.	General Death-rate per thousand.	Smallpox deaths.	General Death-rate per thousand.
1841 ... 1,053	24·2	1863 ... 1,996	24·5
1851 ... 1,062	23·4	1871 ... 7,912	24·6
1855 ... 1,039	24·3	1877 ... 2,551	21·9
Average, 1,051	23·9	Average, 4,153	23·6

To give another illustration, the deaths by Smallpox
in London in 1796 (the highest of the decade) were
3,548, and the whole number of deaths was 19,288. In
1792 the Smallpox deaths were 1,568, and the total
mortality 20,213.

Professor F. W. Newman holds that inasmuch as Smallpox does not affect the total mortality of the community, *that consideration alone* ought to determine the question of Vaccination in Parliament; and that Mr. Taylor and Mr. Hopwood are drawn into confused and useless issues when they leave that firm ground. There is much to be said for Professor Newman's opinion. Perhaps Anti-Vaccinists are somewhat arrogant in their strength. They are ready to encounter Vaccinists any-where, knowing how to smite them hip and thigh from Dan even unto Beersheba. Still war, scientific and effective, is something beyond the joy of battle: it is the application of force to a definite purpose, imposing many restraints upon martial enthusiasm.

XXIX.—MACAULAY AND SMALLPOX.

" Surely the history of this last epidemic tells us most
" clearly that the foe is at our doors, stronger and more
" hostile than it has ever been during this century. It
" is the same form of Smallpox which killed Queen
" Mary, wife of William III., described by Macaulay in
" these terms—

" ' The Plague had visited our shores only once or twice within living
" ' memory, but the Smallpox was always present, filling the churchyard
" ' with corpses, leaving on those whose lives it spared the hideous traces
" ' of its power, turning the babe into a changeling, at which its mother
" ' shuddered, and making the eyes and cheeks of the betrothed maiden
" ' objects of horror to the lover.'

" When Macaulay thus described Smallpox, everyone
" was as subject to it as we are now to Measles, and
" happy were the survivors who passed through with
" unimpaired health or without disfigurement. Now,

" thanks to Vaccination, though its malignity at the
" present time is as great as then, we have, to a large
" extent, protected the population by compulsory laws."

Considering it is claimed for Vaccination that it makes
Smallpox milder, and that the vast majority of our
people have been subjected to its influence, it is sufficiently surprising to learn that " the foe is at our doors,
strong, hostile, and malignant" as in the days when
William III. was King.   The fact we do not dispute.
Smallpox, we believe, is what it ever was, neither milder
nor severer, but qualified as John Hunter taught, and
as Mr. John Simon repeats, by the condition of body of
those who (in consequence of that condition) are open
to attack.

The passage from Macaulay is in frequent requisition
for terrorism, and is in his worst sensational style—a
style which by reason of its systematic untruthfulness
is working his sure perdition as historian.   What exactly
was the prevalence of Smallpox in London toward the
close of the 17th Century is unknown, because Smallpox
and Measles were classed together ; but according to Dr.
Guy in his *250 Years of Smallpox in London*—

" 1.—Epidemics of Smallpox were more frequent in the 18th than in
the 17th Century.
" 2.—The epidemics, taken one with another, were more severe in the
18th than in the 17th Century.
" 3.—The epidemics of the 18th occurred at shorter intervals than those
of the 17th Century.
" 4.—Certain epidemics of the 18th Century lasted more than one year,
but none of the 17th Century.
" 5.—When years of equal, or nearly equal, mortality from all causes
occurring in the 17th and 18th Centuries are compared, deaths by Smallpox are found to furnish a larger contingent of deaths in the 18th than in
the 17th Century.
" These facts afford a strong presumption that Smallpox, for some
reason or other, was a more severe malady in the 18th than in the 17th
Century."

The 18th Century, whether by the practice of inoculation, or by the increase of population and overcrowding in London, was pre-eminently the Smallpox Century; but we put it to any one familiar with its literature, whether the prevalence of the disease excited anything answering to the horror and dismay depicted by Macaulay as characterising the close of the 17th, when Smallpox was less prevalent. The great mass of Smallpox mortality was infantile, about which men and women, sad to say, are generally indifferent; and unless for the occasional damage to the feminine complexion there would have been no more fuss made about Smallpox than there was about Measles, or more deadly fevers. To impute our own alarms and sensibilities to our ancestors is a danger we have always to guard against in our attempts to realise the past.

The deaths from Smallpox of Queen Mary and other notables at home and abroad are continually brought in to point the Vaccination moral; but we ask, to what purpose is the recital? Admitting in full the horrors of London and Parisian Smallpox in high life, what then? They were the appropriate consequences of modes of life, which, however brilliant on the surface, were foul beneath. Queen Mary died of Smallpox, but would Queen Victoria, asked Dr. W. B. Carpenter in discussion, keep away from Buckingham Palace if Smallpox were prevalent in Pimlico? We expect she would; for with the profession of unbounded confidence in the protection of Vaccination, there is nowhere any living faith in its security, and were it non-existent, the dread of the disease could hardly be more intense. As for Queen Mary, we shall not attempt to describe her domestic arrangements. She lived in a palace; but such an atmosphere as pervaded her apartments would revolt the stomach of a modern chambermaid. "Anybody who knows Evelyn," remarked Dr. Carpenter, "knows that he was not a man to be living under bad sanitary conditions, yet his daughter died of Smallpox." Where is the warrant for the assumption? A century intervened between Evelyn and Jenner, and Dr. Carpenter might as reasonably aver that Jenner was not a man to live under bad sanitary conditions, and yet his house at Berkeley was haunted with typhus, and deadly as a Liverpool cellar, or a flat in an Edinburgh close; and yet Jenner had no suspicion that the situation was capable of amendment, but accepted the frequent fever as a dispensation of an inscrutable Providence. Let us beware of anachronisms in sanitary history.

XXX.—Another Summary of Assertion and Contradiction.

"It is the protection afforded by these Compulsory "Laws which it is sought to remove by a Resolution, "concealed in its purpose, but obvious in its design. I "fear that I have wearied the House by statistical "results, but they could not be avoided. To my mind, "they prove conclusively that Smallpox is now as "malignant and loathsome a disease as it was 200 years "ago, and that it is only kept at bay by the protective "influence of Vaccination. This Resolution, if adopted, "would bring us back to the year 1840, by which time "Charity Vaccination had reduced the mortality of "3,000 per million to 600 per million, for I presume it

" would be followed up by another Resolution preventing
" State funds being used for Optional Vaccination.
" Compulsory Vaccination has reduced the mortality,
" including epidemic periods, to one-fourth this amount ;
" but we are to renounce this advantage, because there
" are certain parents who think the law is unjust and
" oppressive."

About Sir Lyon Playfair's statistics, it is unnecessary
to say more. We have shown them to be a handful of
flash notes passed on the credulity and ignorance of the
House of Commons. He knows that his initial statistic
of 3,000 per million is without warrant in fact, and that
the 600 per million statistic does not represent a fall in
Smallpox, but a rise, namely, the great epidemic of
1838-40. We shall not slay the slain. The paragraph
before us is a summary of untruths we have disposed of,
and it suffices that we notify their complete and conclusive contradiction.

XXXI.—THE ARGUMENT FOR COMPULSORY VACCINATION.

" We have many laws interfering with personal liberty.
" We restrict hours of labour to working men, although
" many of them think our restriction unjust. We punish
" the rash traveller who jumps into a train in motion,
" although it would injure no one but himself. If Small-
" pox affected an adult individual only, his right to take
" it could scarcely, however, be disputed. We do not
" punish a man for burning down his own isolated
" mansion if no one is injured but himself. But we do
" punish him if he risk a neighbour's property by his
" act."

Here we have more False Analogies. The enforcement of Vaccination is likened to the restriction of the hours of labour in factories, to the punishment of travellers who jump into trains in motion, and to the prevention of incendiarism. The cases have no resemblance. None seriously complain that their liberty is abridged because they are not allowed to work in factories for more than ten hours a day. None feel it a hardship to be withheld from trains in motion, from injury or death, the shock of fellow passengers, and trouble and annoyance to railway companies. Nor do owners of houses burn them down, but insure them. Such talk is mere talk; talk for the sake of talk to obscure the real issue.

The argument, such as it is, is fatal to Vaccination. It is claimed for the practice that it secures its subjects from Smallpox, and that should the protection "wear out," it may be renewed by Revaccination. Sir Lyon Playfair attests "the Vaccinated rarely perish." Consequently anyone can make himself and his family Smallpox-proof, and for him and his there can be no question of harm from the Unvaccinated. If others like to have Smallpox, let them. If they despise the cheap salvation, they cannot complain when they incur the consequences. Such would be the natural argument if there was any real faith in Vaccination; but there is no real faith. At this day the profession of confidence in Vaccination is little more than make-believe, coupled with mortal dread on the part of those who live and thrive by the practice, first, that the Vaccinated and Revaccinated should catch Smallpox, and second, that the Unvaccinated should multiply and prove themselves as little liable to Smallpox as the Vaccinated, and thus by the double evidence make an end of the imposture and the gains annexed thereto.

It was the promise of Jenner and the primitive Vaccinators that the Vaccinated might live in absolute indifference to Smallpox. That promise has long been exploded. Smallpox was never held in such dread as at the present day, and by none more than the Vaccinated and Revaccinated. The Army and Navy are Revaccinated, and according to doctrine are invulnerable, but we continually see their movements arrested and altered in consequence of outbreaks of Smallpox in this district or in that port; so that an outsider might fairly presume that Vaccination either counted for nothing, or for an extra liability.

Happening lately to drop into a meeting of the St. Pancras Guardians, we heard a discussion on the prosecution of Mr. C. T. Wickham, who on no terms would consent to have his child vaccinated. Mr. Nathan Robinson, a burly and blatant publican, was addressing his associates after this fashion—

"It is said Mr. Wickham should not be prosecuted because he has been already punished. I saw the other day that a woman was had up for being drunk and disorderly the 150th time. What sort of plea would it have been for mercy that she was such an old offender! What would our chairman, Mr. Commissioner Kerr, say to a housebreaker who asked to be excused because he had been convicted ten times already? I should have no objection to Mr. Wickham indulging his preference for Smallpox if he could keep it to himself and his child; but I confess I am afraid of Smallpox. I have been vaccinated, I don't know how often, and shall be again whenever there is occasion; but if Mr. Wickham or his child catches Smallpox, they may give it to me and mine, and I claim that I may be protected in common with the rest of the neighbourhood."

Vaccinated and Revaccinated, and ready to be Vaccinated again, and yet afraid of Smallpox! Fanaticism is detestable, even when it has sincerity behind, but

8

what shall we say of fanaticism that has not even that
poor excuse?   Revaccinated nurses are said to move
about in Smallpox Hospitals with absolute impunity;
yet here was a much-vaccinated St. Pancras Guardian
who said he could not trust himself in the same parish
with an Unvaccinated child!   The fact is obvious.   Mr.
Nathan Robinson, notwithstanding his bluster, has
about as much *real* confidence in Vaccination as Mr.
Wickham himself.   And so it is with other Vaccination
ranters and persecutors.

Mr. A. Milnes has thus put the case in a nutshell—

" Vaccination either—
"I.—Protects you from taking Smallpox; or
"II.—Mitigates Smallpox when you have taken it; or
"III.—Does neither of these things.
"Now, if Vaccination neither protects nor mitigates, then it is useless,
and everyone will admit it ought not to be enforced by law.
"If it only mitigates, then, since the mildest Smallpox is admittedly as
contagious as the most severe, Vaccinated Smallpox is no less dangerous
to the community than Unvaccinated; therefore there is no reason, and
therefore no right, to enforce Vaccination by law.
"If the doctrine is that it protects you from taking Smallpox, those who
believe this doctrine will go and be Vaccinated, and then, being themselves
safe, have no reason, and therefore no right, to enforce Vaccination upon
others by law."

The argument which Sir Lyon Playfair lamely advanced is frequently put in better form thus—" Since we
enforce Education, why not Vaccination?"

The answer is, that none object to Education on any
principle entitled to respect.   If going to school im-
perilled the health and lives of children, compulsion
would be impracticable.   Parents would defy the law,
and public opinion would sustain them in defiance.   But
the limit assigned to compulsion in Education illustrates
the inequity of compulsion as applied to Vaccination.
By general consent, the most important part of educa-

tion is religion; and religion is precisely that part of
Education which is exempted from compulsion. The
law does not even enforce *some* form of religion, so that
the convictions of those parents who regard religion as
a superfluity or superstition may not be aggrieved.
Thus, Education in its highest form is not enforced,
because it is known that if the attempt were made, it
would provoke widespread insurrection. On no terms
could the children of Nonconformists be driven into
Church schools, or the children of Catholics into Nonconformist schools. In short, the theological conscience is
treated with punctilious respect in the matter of Education. Wherever a scruple of conscience is pleaded, there
compulsion is withdrawn.

What, therefore, the opponents of Vaccination demand
is, that the respect thus accorded to the theological
conscience be extended to the scientific conscience. It
is thought intolerable that a child whose parents are
Presbyterians should be taught the Church Catechism,
or that the children of Catholics should be instructed in
Protestant history; or that in public life any disability
should attach to the profession or rejection of any form
of religious belief. We do not dispute the wisdom of
the liberal régime: we merely claim its extension to
scientific convictions—to those, for example, who after
study of Vaccination have arrived at the conclusion that
the operation does nothing to prevent Smallpox, whilst
it frequently inflicts worse mischiefs than the disease it
is supposed to avert. But supposing that Vaccination
were free from danger as leaping over a broomstick,
still those who recognised its inutility would be justified
in resisting its observance. It would be in vain to con-

sole a Baptist, if forced to convey his child to the parish
font, by assuring him that a few drops of water could do
his child no harm.   It is not in human nature to submit
to the indignity of imposture under compulsion ; and to
thousands of Englishmen Vaccination is an imposture,
useless, and dangerous ; and to prosecute and fine them
for faithfulness to their scientific conscience is every
whit as tyrannical as it would be to prosecute and fine
Nonconformists for not going to church, or Catholics for
hearing mass.   There is no difference in the terms of
intolerance ; and, we say it proudly, there is no difference in the spirit with which this tyranny is confronted
and resisted, and that spirit with which liberty in
theology was vindicated and won.   Sometimes it is
advised, as by Dr. Alfred Carpenter, that no parley
should be held with parents, but that their children
should be taken from them and vaccinated in their
despite.   It is unnecessary to stigmatise this advice, but
under such provocation, nothing that is noble in the
story of theological conscience under oppression might
not be repeated.   Vaccination, it may be said, is a small
matter to fight or die for, but where shall we find the
measure of less or more when loyalty to what is known
for right is in question !

———

XXXII.—Contagion and Omissional Infanticide.

   "Every case of Smallpox is a new centre of con-
"tagion.   A man may exercise his own personal taste
"for any disease which he chooses, provided he does not
"injure his neighbours by his idiosyncrasy.   But when

" he produces Omissional Infanticide of his own and his
" neighbours' children by neglect of duty, the State may
" intervene to protect the young population from a fatal
" and mutilative disease. This disease is just as fatal
" and hideous as it was last century, but it has been
" controlled by wise and beneficent laws. Will you
" allow the country to slip back to the period of Vol-
" untary Vaccination, and disseminate many thousands
" of new centres of contagion among the community?
" That is the question which you are asked by the vote
" of to-night to determine."

It is said "every case of Smallpox is a new centre of
contagion," and that "many thousands of new centres
of contagion might be disseminated if the country were
allowed to slip back to Voluntary Vaccination." Dealing
with Smallpox in such terms is resorting once more
to False Analogy. Smallpox is not a fire of which
human beings are fuel. Smallpox is sporadic, and en-
demic, and epidemic; and when epidemic, it has its
rise and fall, and at its height, the so-called centres of
contagion are most numerous, and yet when most
numerous, the epidemic is usually cut short. Is any fire
thus extinguished in the midst of fuel unexhausted?
When Smallpox has broken out and had free course,
such has been the phenomenon; and such also has been
the phenomenon in presence of Vaccination and all the
resources of medical art. We do not offer any explanation; for where we do not know, we try at least to
refrain from the pretence of knowledge.

Whether Smallpox has shown itself amenable to the
control of "wise and beneficent laws," which leave "the
disease just as fatal and hideous as it was last century,"
has been sufficiently discussed. A comparison of the

two great epidemics of the present century, 1838-40 and 1871-72, ought to settle that question. In the first, probably not 30 per cent. of the people were Vaccinated : prior to the second, it was claimed that Vaccination was practically universal, and in Scotland and Ireland had exterminated the disease. Here are the statistics of the two epidemics in England and Wales, which we leave to convey their own lesson.

FIRST EPIDEMIC—1838-40.			SECOND EPIDEMIC—1871-72.		
Years.	Died of Smallpox.	Population.	Years.	Died of Smallpox.	Population.
1838	16,268	15,514,255	1871	23,062	23,095,819
1839	9,131	Average Death-rate per million per annum	1872	19,022	Average Death-rate per million per annum
1840	10,434				
Total,	35,833	772 of three years.	Total,	42,084	918 of two years.

Coming to the political side of the question, we can scarcely do better than refer to an article by Mr. Levy in *The Journal* of the Vigilance Association for July. After showing how incapable is the House of Commons for the discussion of the questions involved in Vaccination, and therefore how completely such a prescription is outside legislative competence, Mr. Levy proceeds—

"But really the *political* question at issue is not whether Vaccination is good or bad. Were we as fully convinced of the cogency of the arguments for Vaccination as we are of the utter fallaciousness of all we have seen or heard, we should still be as far as ever from upholding the compulsory law, or any interference whatever of the State in the matter. The fullest belief in the truth of a proposition does not warrant us in forcing it on others who are not so convinced. Truth requires no such propagandist method, and falsehood does not deserve it. If the question at issue were religious, instead of medical toleration, we would consider any argument for the first article of the Athanasian Creed irrelevant ; for the reason that the utmost that any such argument could do would be to produce conviction, and such conviction could afford no possible justification of persecution. And it is the same with Vaccination. If based on truth, it will prevail without the aid of the policeman. If based on falsehood, exaggeration, or superstition, such aid will tend to keep it in existence long after the natural term of its life has closed. If the majority which enforces on the minority a particular mode of treatment for their children had examined the matter for themselves, it would be bad enough. But they have not done so. They have accepted the dogma on the authority of their doctors, who themselves have accepted it from a small body of specialists, who are paid advocates of the system."

Concerning the crime of Omissional Infanticide, this is Mr. Levy's commentary—

"Sir Lyon Playfair had another plea for compulsion—or at least another phrase. 'By Vaccination we operated on children who could not protect themselves, in order to save them from Omissional Infanticide.' Omissional Infanticide is good. It means that A and B are justified in compelling C to give his child a disease—perhaps more than one, from the effects of which it may die ; because, if it had not that disease, it might have another, and if it had that other disease, it might end fatally. This is Omissional Infanticide. But why is not Sir Lyon Playfair logical for once, if only by way of diversion ? Infanticide is murder by the law of England. Why not propose that parents who refuse to give their children Cowpox shall be hanged ? Persons certainly should not be allowed to kill their children ; and to propose a small fine as a penalty for such a crime is a ludicrous piece of barbarism. We ask the compulsionists to choose which horn of the dilemma they prefer—either they are right, and should give parents the alternative of the lancet or the rope : or they are wrong, and should give up a system of petty persecution which confessedly is valueless, even for the purpose for which it was intended by the imperious and dogmatic practitioners of the most empirical of arts."

XXXIII.—LAW AS TO "OMISSIONAL INFANTICIDE."

If refusal to vaccinate is Omissional Infanticide, the crime is not only tolerated, but individuals and societies spare no pains to encourage and multiply it. For, be it noted, whilst Vaccination is nominally compulsory, it is not really so for those who have the courage to defy or the art to evade the law.

Members of Parliament usually pride themselves on being practical men, who do not concern themselves with theories but with realities. To such we say, There are thousands of parents in this country who will not suffer their children to be vaccinated. They may be prosecuted, fined, and imprisoned, *ad libitum*, but it is certain they will never submit. Legislate as you please, they will set your legislation at defiance. Nor by any measure can you overcome their resistance, for public opinion will not sanction their subjugation *vi et armis*. As it is, the law is continually checked in its application by the scandal and disapprobation it excites.

Having, then, an irreducible insurrection on hand—an insurrection, too, that is yearly acquiring volume and extension, What should be done? Sometimes it is asked, Would you recommend surrender to insurgents? but the question implies that insurgents are subdued under the existing administration of the law. That, however, is precisely what is not accomplished. A parent says he will not have his child vaccinated. He may be prosecuted and fined a dozen times, until the patience of his prosecutors is exhausted; and then surrender takes place under ignominious conditions. The child is not vaccinated, and before the community the parent appears in the double character of martyr and victor. And this transaction is under continual repetition, to the grave discredit of justice; and as the law is administered, the result is unavoidable.

Poor Law Guardians who are responsible for the enforcement of Vaccination often experience painful humiliation in having their authority flouted by those who hold the rite in contempt, and occasionally appeal to the Local Government Board for counsel and comfort. The advice of the Board is usually conveyed in a copy of what is called the Evesham Letter, addressed to the Guardians of that Union, 17th September, 1875. Summarily, the advice is—" Do not prosecute to the extent of persecution. Consider well whether insistence is likely to result in success. If not—why, then leave off!" In a word—Surrender to irreducible insurrection. This advice has been stigmatised with many opprobrious epithets; but what other advice could be tendered? Let any one try to define an alternative. If a parent will not have his child vaccinated after three fines he is not likely to submit after thirty; and what Guardians, other than hotheaded fools, would engage in conflict so useless? Many Guardians have interpreted the Evesham Letter liberally — as we daresay was intended. Having prosecuted once they prosecute no more. Others go further. Satisfied, on the report of their vaccination officer, that certain ratepayers will not have their children vaccinated on any terms, they discreetly leave them alone, arguing "What is the use of incurring trouble, exciting offence, and encouraging opposition—and all for naught!"

Another difficulty supervenes. Guardians may prosecute, but it is magistrates who pronounce judgment; and as the law concedes the widest discretion to the Bench, and justices entertain various opinions as to the expediency of enforced Vaccination, and its application in particular cases, penalties are multiform, sometimes 1s., sometimes 2s. 6d., sometimes 5s., sometimes 10s., and so on; with occasional dismissals for irregular procedure on the part of prosecutors and for "reasonable, excuse" on the part of the prosecuted. Guardians naturally lose heart when they are not only disobeyed, but when the disobedient are let off cheaply. Frequently, however, the zeal of the Guardians meets with corresponding zeal on the Bench; the utmost penalty,

and the utmost costs are inflicted; and the medical
nonconformist is crushed as it were between the upper
and nether millstone; and when this process is repeated
again and again, with malignity on the one side and
fanaticism on the other, it is easy to imagine the exas-
peration which is created. Indeed, when a poor parent
is prosecuted and fined repeatedly and relentlessly
because he refuses to yield up his child to what he
is convinced is a useless and dangerous operation,
knowing, moreover, that in other parishes the same
"offence" is either passed over or lightly dealt with, a
cruel strain is put upon his loyalty. In the name of
law, a wrong is inflicted which all just men recognise as
insufferable.

Such outrageous irregularities in the administration
of the law are beyond defence. No one ventures to
maintain that it is just to prosecute a poor man to ruin
with fines, which a man in better circumstances pays
with indifference, and secures immunity by payment.
Alike by Conservatives and Liberals the scandal of the
situation has been recognised and deplored. When the
present Government came into power in 1880, Mr.
Dodson introduced a Bill to limit the punishment for
refusal to vaccinate to a definite penalty, but such was
the outcry raised against the measure by the medical
trade unions that it was withdrawn. As asserted in
their organ, the *British Medical Journal*, of 17th July,
1880, "If the law were thus changed it would become a
dead letter," in apparent ignorance of the fact that over
extensive areas the law is thus changed; and, further,
that in towns like Dewsbury and Keighley, where opponents of Vaccination are sufficiently numerous, the

law is so broken down that none are troubled with Vaccination who dislike it, whilst nobody is a whit the worse for the non-observance of the rite. The withdrawal of Mr. Dodson's Bill was attended with many regrets. Mr. Bright, writing to Mr. B. Sharpe, of Middleton, on 21st September, 1880, said—

"I am sorry the Government Vaccination Bill did not pass. It would have been a great relief, and was an eminently just measure."

Many opponents of Vaccination were of a different mind, saying, "The more outrageously a bad law is " administered, the more complete will be its destruc-" tion. Nothing has piled such odium on Vaccination " as these multiplied penalties for its refusal. They " have excited inquiry; they have created resistance; " and they have begotten such sympathy for sufferers " among the indifferent, that it has become possible to " reduce the law to a dead letter in many quarters. " We certainly can have no interest in putting a bad " law into such form as its admirers think equitable. " Far better leave the law as it is, with its injustice to " work for us, and hasten the day when we shall get rid " of the whole thing."

The question remains, "Why should a parent be fined even 6d. because he refuses to have his child vaccinated?" It is sometimes answered, as by Sir Lyon Playfair, "There is no reason whatever why he should not indulge his preference for Smallpox, but the safety of others has to be considered." But, as we have asked, Wherein does he jeopardise the safety of others if the claim made for Vaccination be valid? Vaccination, it is said, protects its subjects from Smallpox, and so thoroughly, that vaccinated nurses in Smallpox Hospitals move about in the variolous atmosphere unharmed. The Unvaccinated cannot, therefore, be a source of harm to the Vaccinated, secure under the charm of the Jennerian rite. To assert that the Unvaccinated are a peril to the Vaccinated is to deny that Vaccination is a defence against Smallpox, and the more vehemently the assertion is made, the more flagrantly is distrust in Vaccination proclaimed.

It is sometimes said that Vaccination is a medical question, and occasionally medical men refuse to discuss it with laymen as outside their province ; but all questions are transformed when they ascend into politics. The origin, character, and action of varieties of animal virus are mysteries, and may remain mysteries with general indifference ; but when it is claimed that the inoculation of such virus prevents Smallpox, and that whoever refuses to submit his child to the said inoculation shall be fined 20s., *then* the matter is brought within the jurisdiction of every citizen, and he becomes entitled to information, to the exercise of his judgment and the expression of his opinion. As a mystery Vaccination belongs to experts ; but as a Parliamentary preventive of Smallpox, it is within the discrimination of all who can observe and appreciate the evidence of numbers. " Is Vaccination a preventive of Smallpox ? " asks Dr. W. A. Guy, and replies, " *To this question there is, there can be, no answer except such as is couched in the language of figures.*" The value of Vaccination is, therefore, not a medical but a statistical question, and can be determined in no other way.

But whether a medical question, Anti-Vaccinists have studied and mastered it. None know more of Vaccination, its history, transformations, varieties, and consequences ; and nothing apparently is more exasperating to medical men than the discovery that an increasing body of laymen throughout the country know more of their mystery than they know themselves, and who trip them up and expose their defective knowledge and mis-statements whenever they open their mouths. " Define your pox, sir," is a demand which of itself is apt to take the breath out of an apologist for Vaccination; for until the pox is defined, he is nowhere, Vaccination being of several incompatible varieties. This aggressive attitude concerning the interiors of "the mystery" is becoming more and more pronounced, and Vaccinators find themselves exposed to a fire of criticism for which they are ill-prepared. Dr. W. B. Carpenter, with a hardihood the discreeter order of medical men little approve, recently came forth as the champion of Vaccination, and by Mr. Taylor has been met and overthrown. Mr. Taylor's refutation has been spread over the whole earth. It is a hand-book to the controversy, making converts wherever read ; and we may fairly say it is unanswered because unanswerable. Vaccination a mystery for experts! It will soon lie an open secret, unscientific in origin, empirical in development, sordid in defence. The controversy widens in the press, and in any newspaper where discussion has free course, the opponents of Vaccination bear down their adversaries with the weight of evidence and argument. It is the same in public meetings and debating clubs. Almost everywhere, when the question of Compulsory Vaccination is put to the vote, the majority go against compulsion. Indeed, the advocates of enforced Vaccination would find it hard to hold a public meeting anywhere and carry a vote in their favour. There is an opinion forming in the country which will surprise and perplex many candidates for Parliament. Presently they will have to face the entire disestablishment and disendowment of Vaccination, when the practice will take its place with bleeding, blistering, and salivation—medical fads equally reputable and authoritative, but which, without establishment and endowment, like many similar renowned and life-saving fads, have had their day and ceased to be. Medicine has fashions as irrational, irresistible, and transitory as millinery; and Vaccination has simply been preserved from the common lot by the intervention of protective legislation.

Sufferers from evil law are sometimes told, that whilst they are free to use appropriate means to get the law repealed, they ought to obey it while it exists. The answer is, that as long as they obey the law nobody will stir to get it altered. But in this matter of Vaccination there is no choice. When a parent has discovered the imposture of Vaccination and its perils, or has had, or has seen, some dear child injured or killed by the disgusting and degrading superstition, his duty becomes unquestionable. For him, the mandate of the Highest is disobedience, inflexible disobedience, and the propagation of disobedience. Herein is our power as Anti-Vaccinists. We are entrenched in the enlightened intelligence of mankind, and in the tenderest and deepest and strongest affections of the human heart. Toward the evil law we are Irreconcileables. Whilst it exists, we fight, and call others to the contest with the firm assurance that the issue must be victory. "Where the law comes into conflict with the conscience of man," says Mr. John Morley, "it is the law that should be altered, and not conscience that should be forced "—but conscience that is worth the name cannot be forced.

Nor are we merely aggressive and destructive. Our work is educational. In teaching our countrymen to distrust and abhor a charm against Smallpox, we continually invite them to place their confidence without reserve in the true specifics against all zymotic disease— in cleanliness of person and habitation, in pure air and water and wholesome food.

A WORD FOR SIR LYON PLAYFAIR.

EDINBURGH, 9*th November*, 1883.

DEAR WHITE,—It was said that no man could be so wise as Lord Thurlow looked; and I may parody the observation and say that no man so intelligent as Sir Lyon Playfair can be so foolish as you make him. I have read your discussion of his speech carefully, but it is written throughout under a misapprehension. You treat Sir Lyon as if he were speaking his own mind when he is speaking the mind of his constituents. He is no more to be held personally responsible for his speech than is a barrister for his defence of a gang of swindlers. The advocate may know his clients are swindlers, but it is his business to set their case in the best light, and to win a verdict in their favour if he can.

Sir Lyon is the delegate of the Universities of Edinburgh and St. Andrews. The majority of *his* electors are medical men, whose livelihood and professional pride are associated with Vaccination; and he

could not possibly commend himself more effectually to
their continued favour than by a rattling speech in
defence of their practice. Nay, we may look at it in
another way. If he had not shown himself ready to
encounter Mr. Taylor's motion, or worse, had he shown
any hesitation in toeing the outer line of cowpox
orthodoxy, take my word for it, he would have lost his
seat at the next election ; and no one realises this more
acutely than Sir Lyon himself. He was elected in 1880
by a majority of 74 in a constituency of 6,039, of whom
2,522 voted for him and 2,448 for Mr. Bickersteth ; it
being well known that his chief support was derived from
the medical wing of the constituency. He exists as M.P.
for Edinburgh and St. Andrews with a rope round his
neck, and if he manifested the least self-will in his treatment of medical questions he would be slung aloft without
mercy or hesitation. He may disport himself at pleasure
in the political arena, but within the medical circle, it
is for him to recognise his subjection. There is no
despotism so exacting and pitiless as that of a trade-
union.

Some may wonder where men can be found to submit
to such restraints, but what will they not suffer for the
most trumpery political distinction ? If Sir Lyon's seat
were vacant, there would be a score to leap into it. Sir
Lyon is ambitious, but he is no longer young, and
cannot start afresh. His hopes have often drawn near
fulfilment, but have been cruelly quenched. He was
once Postmaster-General for a month or two, but some-
how he has stuck fast in mediocrity. Had he been an
Irishman, he would either have been in the cabinet, or
elevated and extinguished in a peerage ; but the lib-

eralism of Scotland is so assured that its representatives are passed over with familiar indifference. Instead of statesmanship, Sir Lyon is called to the defence of cowpox, and is rewarded with the adulation of Sir Charles Dilke.

Universities are multiplying over the land, and the question of their general representation in Parliament must soon be raised. It seems to me the expediency of such representation is extremely doubtful. M.P.'s for universities are nominees of trading professions, chiefly clerical and medical. The typical university M.P. is dull and docile, holding his place by abject subservience. Even Oxford threw over Sir Robert Peel and Mr. Gladstone whenever they preferred patriotism to clericalism. However we may contrive, men will enter Parliament to promote ends which are sectional rather than national, but it is against good policy to construct constituencies which by the law of their being will select members to do so. As one who respects Sir Lyon Playfair, I grudge to see his undoubted abilities thrown away and discredited in the advocacy of the trading interests of the medical graduates of Edinburgh and St. Andrews.—Yours truly,

LAURIE MACKENZIE.

SIR CHARLES DILKE'S SPEECH.

SIR CHARLES DILKE'S speech is printed with Sir Lyon Playfair's, and to complete our task it may be well to take it to pieces in the same manner. Sir Charles expresses himself with the recklessness of inexperience. It is not supposed that he knows anything more of Vaccination than M.P.'s in general or Mr. Henry Richard in particular. Moreover, it is the habit of the President of the Local Government Board to speak on Vaccination as inspired by the medical officials of the department; and in answering questions thereon in Parliament, we can usually discern the tactics of the prompters behind, excusing or denying the mishaps of the practice, as under circumstances may be considered most expedient. Some Presidents make better mediums than others. Mr. Dodson, Sir Charles Dilke's predecessor, repeated his instructions automatically, and in a case like that of the Algerian Disaster went through a course of prevarication which would have been unaccountable on any personal hypothesis. Sometimes, as in the instance of Mr. Robert Lowe (Lord Sherbrooke), a spokesman has intensified his inspiration. Thus Mr. Lowe assured the House of Commons in 1861 that the sacrifice of a clause in the Vaccination Act of 1859 to please Mr. Duncombe "had occasioned the loss of thousands of lives," for which "he had suffered bitter reflections"—the reflections, if

like the lost lives, being wholly imaginary. It is not
probable that Sir Charles Dilke will show himself as
passive as Mr. Dodson, or develop his instructions with
the license of Mr. Lowe, but he has made a beginning
that does not promise well for the future. Mr. P. A.
Taylor, in the course of his speech on 19th June, described the position, and gave him honest warning,
saying—

"There is, I admit, one small portion of the medical
" profession of whose conversion I entertain no hope
" whatever, and that is the small body of highly paid
" medical gentlemen who sit behind the throne of the
" President of the Local Government Board, and who
" are more powerful on these matters than is the Presi-
" dent of the Local Government Board himself. They
" are, I have not the slightest doubt, honourable and
" intelligent men, but they are men whose *raison d'être*
" is Vaccination, and they can no more be expected to
" question its excellence than can the bench of bishops
" question the Thirty-nine Articles. They are irrespon-
" sible in the advice they give, or they are only respon-
" sible to the President of the Local Government Board.
" My right hon. friend has probably not studied very
" deeply the question of Vaccination. It is natural that
" he should not have done so, and if I may be permitted
" to say from the answers he has given in this House, I
" should assume certainly that he had not done so
" (laughter). But surely it is most unfortunate and
" painful to be made the mouthpiece of a set of medical
" experts upon doctrines as to which they have and can
" have no valid opinion of their own."

Let Sir Charles Dilke pluck up courage to distrust his
Whitehall advisers, and apply his mind to the Vaccination Question for himself. He may then revert with
anything but pleasure to his performance on the night

of 19th June in support of Sir Lyon Playfair; but he will have the satisfaction, which falls to the lot of every progressive statesman, of finding himself wiser with his own eyes than he ever could be with the eyes of interested counsellors.

To the examination of the speech of Sir Charles Dilke let us now address ourselves.

I.—HARMLESS HERE, HARMFUL THERE.

"My two Hon. Friends, the Members for Leicester " and Stockport, have used language so violent with " regard to the effects of Vaccination that my own " feeling when listening to them has been one of aston- " ishment—astonishment that having been frequently " vaccinated myself, I should find myself alive to tell the " tale."

We often learn with surprise what of ourselves we should never have suspected; and thus of Sir Charles Dilke's solicitude for his complexion, and the sufferings and risks he has undergone for its preservation. Still the sufferings and risks may have been minimised for him. There is Vaccination *and* Vaccination; and the rite as administered to a person of quality may differ widely from that thought good enough for a pauper's brat. It has also to be remembered that the same Vaccination which may not harm one or many, may harm another or others. The constitutions to be poisoned have to be reckoned with as well as the character of the virus. There is no commoner fallacy than the reverse opinion that children vaccinated alike will do well or ill alike; and if, therefore, some do well, it is proof conclusive that Vaccination is not the source of mischief in those who do ill. As Dr. Alfred Carpenter stated at Brighton in 1880—

" It has been established by undoubted experiments that the cultivation of morbid matter may convert what was at first a comparatively harmless secretion into a virulent material capable of generating acute disease."

Here we have one of the chief perils of Vaccination defined. It is vain to speak of Vaccine Virus as harmless in presence of such "undoubted experiments." If what is a comparatively harmless secretion at one moment may, by transfer to another organism, be converted into a virulent material, capable of generating acute disease, many of the disasters of Vaccination are accounted for ; and not only accounted for, but proved to be beyond foresight and prevention.

II.—An Ecstatic Compliment.

"My Hon. Friends have been so completely and " crushingly answered upon the statistical side of their " statement by my Right Hon. Friend, Sir Lyon Play- " fair that I need only briefly allude to that side of the " question. The House has often the advantage of " hearing my Right Hon. Friend upon scientific subjects, " but I do not think we have ever had a greater treat in " the way of a scientific exposition than that which he " has afforded us to-night."

It would have been a pity to have missed the lesson of this compliment. The light it throws on the capacity of him who bestowed it, the House which cheered it, and the grace and truth of its blushing recipient is profitable for instruction and remembrance. The vendor of a parcel of bogus statistics and a commentary rotten with untruth was told that he had produced a complete and crushing answer to speeches whose positions he left

untouched, and that the House of Commons never had
a greater treat in the way of scientific exposition!
Poor House of Commons!

III.—ALTERNATIONS IN DISEASE.

" The Hon. Members for Leicester and Stockport have
" spoken a great deal of the effect of improved sanitary
" conditions on the suppression of Smallpox, but on con-
" trasting three successive periods—namely, between
" 1841 and 1853, the Optional Period; between 1854
" and 1871, which was spoken of as the Obligatory
" Period; and between 1872 and 1880, or the Compul-
" sory Period—they would find that the decline had
" been chiefly among children under ten years of age.
" The reduction of the death-rate from Smallpox, as
" between the first and third periods, was from 100 to
" 51 in people of all ages, and from 100 to 20 in the case
" of children under five years of age. The corresponding
" reduction in other causes of death had been from 100
" to 93 in people of all ages, and from 100 to 94 in cases
" of children under five years old."

Smallpox, as we have pointed out, is chiefly a disease
of the young; at some times and in some countries it
has been almost exclusively so. Consequently, when
Smallpox falls off, the decline is most conspicuous among
the more numerous class of sufferers. Latterly, Smallpox, in common with other forms of zymotic disease,
has exhibited a tendency to attack a higher range of
ages. The causes of such alternations in disease we
understand as little as those of the weather and the
seasons; and in so far as they leave the death-rate unaffected, they are of little practical importance.

IV.—INOCULATION AND SMALLPOX.

" In last Century the death-rate from Smallpox was

" slightly increased by Inoculation ; but when Vaccina-
" tion began to be practised at the beginning of the
" present Century, the mortality fell with astonishing
" rapidity.   Therefore it is impossible to argue with any
" approach to truth that the great mortality of the last
" Century was owing to Inoculation."

If the Smallpox mortality of last Century was not
largely due to the practice of Inoculation with Smallpox, to what was it due?   Was it without cause?   Also,
why was it greater than in the preceding, the 17th
Century?   Whoever holds that Inoculation did little to
increase Smallpox, is bound to maintain that Smallpox
is not diffused by infection—an opinion the reverse of
what is prevalent at this day.   The fact that Inoculators
like Dimsdale insisted on keeping their patients in strict
seclusion ; that Jenner and the early Vaccinators held
they could never conquer Smallpox until its artificial
propagation was forbidden ; and that the Act of 1840
constituted Inoculation a penal offence—all point to the
conclusion that Smallpox must have bred and multiplied
Smallpox.   Sir Charles Dilke thinks otherwise, and we
own there is something to be said in his favour.   When
Inoculation was most extensively practised toward the
close of last Century, then Smallpox began to fall off,
and Vaccination, subsequently introduced, had the credit
of the fall ; although it was not even pretended that the
classes who chiefly suffer from Smallpox had the benefit
of the Jennerian rite otherwise than vicariously.   " The
mortality from Smallpox," says Sir Charles, " fell off
with astonishing rapidity at the beginning of the present
Century."   We allow that it did ; at the same time
insisting that the fall set in before and continued
irrespective of Vaccination : adding, that in so far as the

fall was not related to sanitary improvement, cognate factors of death took the place of Smallpox, as shown by Dr. Watt in the instance of Glasgow, and generally confirmed and explained by Dr. Farr.

V.—KILMARNOCK SMALLPOX.

" In the early part of last Century a schoolmaster in
" Kilmarnock kept a very careful register of every death
" and the cause of it in the district.   That register has
" been most elaborately examined, and it is found that
" the death-rate in Kilmarnock from Smallpox—there
" being no Inoculation—was twenty times greater than
" at present for people of all ages, and of children under
" five years old, thirty-five times greater than it is now."

What is intended by this reference to Kilmarnock is not easy to make out.   None dispute that Smallpox was a predominant variety of febrile disease last Century: whilst nevertheless it is necessary to assert its limitations and compensations.   Leprosy was once a common disease, but leprosy passed away.   Ague used to be the curse of life over extensive English areas, but gradually disappeared as drainage developed.   If we knew with precision the conditions that favour Smallpox, we might explain how it happened to wax and wane with the 18th Century.

Dr. M'Vail has published the schoolmaster's register of Kilmarnock mortality during 36 years, 1728-64; from which it appears that outbreaks of Smallpox occurred at intervals of about 4½ years, resulting in 622 deaths—

"Of these 622 deaths in 36 years, only 3 occurred in people over 20 years of age. . . . Of 45 children who succumbed in the epidemic of 1733, 44 were less than 4 years 8 months old, the 45th being aged 7.   Thus only 1 child that died in the 1733 epidemic had been alive in the previous epidemic of 1728."

To be secure from Smallpox in old Kilmarnock, it therefore sufficed to be no longer a child.

Kilmarnock suffered severely from Smallpox. The total deaths from all causes, 1728-64, were 3,860, of which, as said, 622 were attributed to Smallpox, or 16 per cent. In Edinburgh, at the same period, the rate for Smallpox was no more than 10 per cent.; but in Glasgow, toward the close of the Century, it was 20 per cent.—all alike infantile mortality. Dr. M'Vail describes the disease as exciting terror in Kilmarnock, saying— "One can barely imagine what must have been the feelings of a mother regarding these fearful visitations"—an extraordinary misapprehension of the temper of the time. Smallpox excited as little dismay then as Measles at this day. The disease was accepted as an ordinance of Providence which it would have been foolish and impious to resent. Sir Charles Dilke says Inoculation was not practised, but that is far from certain. Not only were no attempts made to limit the extension of the disease, but its infection was courted as an inconvenience it was good policy to incur and have done with. As for the loss of children, it was endured with more equanimity than tender hearts may be willing to allow, as an anecdote from Sir Archibald Alison may illustrate. Sir Patrick Grant, on his return from India, went to visit a woman, old and infirm, who had tended him in infancy. "Well, Mary," said Sir Patrick, "how many children have you had?" "Troth, sir, I have borne my gudeman *thirteen*." "Thirteen! How in the world did you contrive to bring up so many?" "Oh, sir, ye see the Lord was rale merciful, for aye as *He sent ane, He took awa' the tither;* so we jist hirpilt through."

Dr. M'Vail further describes " the children who recovered from Smallpox as growing up disfigured for life "—an occasional sequence of the disease, but absurdly untrue of the majority of sufferers.

Unfortunately, the population of Kilmarnock is unknown at the time in question. It may have been 3,350 or 4,200. The latter figure would give an average annual death-rate of about 24 per thousand ; not differing widely from that of contemporary Kilmarnock with 24,000 inhabitants. Dr. M'Vail is exultant over the decline of Smallpox, and fancies he has made a discovery for the discomfiture of Mr. P. A. Taylor and his adherents ; but if people die as fast in new as in old Kilmarnock, wherein is the advantage ? It may be preferable to die of any disease rather than Smallpox, but that is matter of taste. Were it otherwise, however ; were the death-rate of old Kilmarnock greater than that of new Kilmarnock, the fact would merely indicate worse conditions of existence. Life is only extensible in so far as improvement is effected in the conditions of life. Forms of disease are subject to modification ; some of them are probably convertible and interchangeable; one form comes and another goes, but conditions remaining the same, the crop of death is equal. Hence Mr. Edwin Chadwick's sagacious advice—

"Keep your eye on the death-rate. Let nothing short of its reduction satisfy you. There may be no startling outbreak of this fever or that fever; but if the death-rate is unabated there can be no improvement that ought to satisfy you. The death-rate is the test of sanitary progress. Keep, therefore, your eye on the death-rate."

VI.—THE NURSES WHO NEVER CATCH SMALLPOX.

" The Hon. Member for Leicester has attempted to " disprove the statement that the most carefully revac-

" cinated class, namely, the nurses in Smallpox Hospitals,
" were absolutely free from Smallpox, although exposed
" to the greatest possible danger; and he stated that
" some of them had died. I am prepared to say my
" Hon. Friend has been misinformed. No case has been
" known among the nurses of the London Smallpox
" Hospital, and there have been only three slight cases
" among the nurses of the Metropolitan Asylums Board.
" It is notorious to every medical man, and to Hon.
" Members, that persons exposed to so high a degree of
" contagion must certainly have contracted Smallpox in
" considerable numbers and died had they not been pro-
" tected by Vaccination."

If it were so, how shall we explain the immunity of
nurses which was notorious before Vaccination was
heard of? and the equal immunity of nurses at this day
who have declined Revaccination?—as proved by Mr.
Taylor from Paris and Dublin.

When it is claimed that Revaccination saves nurses
from Smallpox, the claim in its extravagance defeats
itself: For, if it is Revaccination which saves nurses
under the highest exposure to Smallpox, why does it
fail to save soldiers, sailors, policemen, and other equally
revaccinated persons whose exposure is much less
intense? Everyone must recognise the fallacy involved
in an assertion so unqualified, and perceive that if nurses
do not contract Smallpox it must be for some reason
outside their Vaccination or Revaccination.

A nurse in a Smallpox Hospital, it is scarcely necessary to observe, is not an ordinary woman. If she
selects such repulsive work for herself, her selection is a
discrimination of character; and her appointment by
those who are not likely to favour feeble or sensitive
organisations, is an additional guarantee of that vigour

and hardness, which, beyond aught else, withstand the aggression of disease.

Then we have to remember that Smallpox, once almost exclusively an infantile disease, remains predominantly an affection of the young. Wherefore, nurses, as adult or middle-aged women, have their risk of Smallpox prodigiously reduced by reason of their years.

Again, many nurses in Smallpox Hospitals have entered as patients, and in default of other occupation have accepted service.

Lastly, something is to be attributed to what may be called seasoning or acclimatisation. If a woman engaged as a nurse endures the hospital atmosphere for a week, she may be taken as proof against Smallpox for any term; the courage acquired from immunity constituting an additional safeguard. If, on the contrary, a new hand succumbs, she is not reckoned among nurses, but takes rank as a patient; the explanation being that "she must have entered with Smallpox in the incubative stage"—a stage with convenient limits.

It is, therefore, easy to see how nurses on these terms escape Smallpox, or should they contract it, how easily the difficulty is got out of. Sometimes it is asked, why nurses escape Smallpox and yet fall victims to Typhus. The answer is that Typhus attacks a higher range of ages; and that a truer comparison would run with nurses in contact with Scarlatina, Whooping-Cough, and Measles.

Mr. Taylor observed that nurses do not always escape Smallpox, and he might have adduced a variety of instances in proof. Sir Charles Dilke tried to turn the

observation by saying that Mr. Taylor "had been misinformed," for no case of death "had been known among
the nurses of the London Smallpox Hospital, and only
three slight cases among the nurses of the Metropolitan
Asylums Board." But Mr. Taylor did not limit his
observation to London; where, let us add, if a nurse
died, no pains would be spared to hush up the scandal,
or to assign her death to any cause other than Smallpox.

VII.—THE LONDON POSTMEN.

"Then in the case of the persons permanently em-
"ployed in the postal service in London—averaging
"10,504, who are required to undergo Vaccination on
"admission, unless it has been performed within seven
"years, there has not been a single death from Small-
"pox between 1870 and 1880, which period included
"the Smallpox epidemic, and there has been only ten
"slight cases of the disease. In the Telegraphic
"Department, where there is not so complete an en-
"forcement of Vaccination, there have only been twelve
"cases in a staff averaging 1,500 men."

Had there not been a single case of Smallpox among
the officers of the London Post Office we should not
have been surprised ; and that their immunity should be
ascribed to their Vaccination is one of those daring
drafts upon public credulity which are successful by
reason of their daring. As Dr. Littledale observes—

"It is noticeable that whereas the trained and logical intellect requires
that the proof shall be always proportionate to the magnitude of the thing
to be proved, there is a very large class of minds for which audacious
assertion has such a fascination, that if only the assertion be daring enough,
no other proof is desired."

It goes without saying that the postman's calling is
an extremely healthy one. He has abundant exercise

in the open air, and, the discipline of the office being strict, his life is regular beyond that of most working men. Starting with a good constitution, maintained by exercise and sober habits, and past the age when Small-pox is most prevalent, why should the postman be otherwise than exempt from what even in London is a comparatively rare form of disease? In the great epidemic of 1871 there perished 7,912 Londoners, re-presenting, say, 50,000 cases of Smallpox; but the population of London in that year was 3,263,872, from which, deducting 50,000, we have 3,213,872 who escaped unharmed. Yet are we invited to wonder and admire because the great goddess, Vaccinia, preserved ten or twelve thousand postmen and telegraphists in the over-whelming majority of three millions and odd!

Mr. Herbert Spencer, in his *Study of Sociology*, makes a happy use of the epidemic of 1871 in illustration of the mode in which fear affects the judgment: he writes—

"An instance in which dread destroys the balance of judgment was thrust upon my attention during the Smallpox Epidemic, which so unac-countably spread after twenty years of Compulsory Vaccination. A lady living in London, sharing in the general trepidation, was expressing her fears to me. I asked whether, if she lived in a town of twenty thousand inhabitants and heard of one person dying of Smallpox in the course of a week, she would be much alarmed. Naturally, she answered no; and her fears were somewhat calmed when I pointed out that, taking the whole population of London and the number of deaths per week from Smallpox, this was about the rate of mortality at that time caused by it. Yet in other minds, as in her mind, panic had produced an entire incapacity for forming a rational estimate of the peril. Nay, indeed, so perturbing was the emo-tion, that an unusual amount of danger to life was imagined at a time when the danger to life was smaller than usual; for the returns showed that the mortality from all causes was rather below the average than above it. While the evidence proved that the risk of death was less than common, this wave of feeling which spread through society produced an irresistible conviction that it was uncommonly great."

It may be said, the postman has to deliver letters at infected houses, but at how many such houses? Smallpox, at the worst, is never diffused over London, and the poor folk who suffer from the disease have few dealings with the post-office. Here, for example, is a summary from the Registrar-General of the place of death of the 475 persons who died of Smallpox in London, in the course of 1880—

Districts.			Deaths from Smallpox.			In Hospitals and Workhouses.
North	...	...	185	...	...	176
Central	...	...	4	...	...	2
South	...	...	166	...	...	160
East	...	...	67	...	...	34
West	...	...	53	...	...	53
			475			425

Thus of 475, no more than 50 died in their own beds. The statement bears its lesson on its face. Yet we are invited to believe that letters and telegrams were delivered and received from these poor people, and that their bearers were preserved from catching their Smallpox, because they were revaccinated!

But supposing it had been otherwise, and that Smallpox had been a genteel disease most frequent in Mayfair and Belgravia, would the delivery and collection of letters have communicated it? If the testimony of those who are responsible for Smallpox Hospitals is worth a straw, the very suggestion is absurd. Why, even sanitary officers who, like postmen, move in the open air, but unlike postmen, come into contact with disease, enjoy exemption from infection. It may be vain for us to try to inspire a rational temper into those who like to terrify and to be terrified (a numerous body); but they can scarcely disregard the authority of a faithful Vaccinist like Dr. Henry D. Littlejohn, of Edinburgh, Medical Officer to the Scots Board of Health. In the Annual Report for Scotland, 1879-80, he thus delivers himself of advice, the fruit of twenty-five years of active sanitary service. Mark his words—

"All medical authorities are agreed that the risk attending the entering a room in which there are cases of infectious disease is infinitesimally small *to the healthy individual;* and that even where a person actually assists in removing a patient sick of an infectious disorder to another apartment or to a conveyance, while the risk is greater, it is in reality *very small to the sound constitution.*

"As a rule, it is rare to find nurses affected who live for hours and days at a time in the same atmosphere with the sick, and who at the same time make use of the simplest precautions. It is still rarer to hear of medical men sickening of infectious diseases caught in their practice, and it is well known that medical men never, or very rarely, bring the infection of such diseases to their households.

"For twenty-five years I have been engaged in active sanitary work, and have had, with very limited staff, to cope with serious outbreaks of Cholera, Smallpox, Fever, Scarlatina, Measles, and Whooping Cough, and although I have, during that period, brought up a large family, I have never communicated any of these diseases to my children or dependents, nor am I aware that any of the numerous Sanitary Inspectors who have acted under me have ever contracted or communicated these diseases while in the public service.

"To live in the constant dread of infection is one of the surest methods of courting the risk of an attack. It is a popular, and I believe a true, saying with regard to Cholera, that the fear of it kills more than the scourge itself. *This holds equally good of other forms of infection;* and the Sanitary Inspector, to be an efficient public servant, must be assured of this cardinal fact, *that infectious germs of all kinds have no power of successfully attacking the healthy individual.*"

A piece of valid experience like this is worth yards of argumentative disquisition ; and in its light is seen how preposterous is the assertion that London postmen are saved from Smallpox by reason of their Revaccination. Of course Sir Charles Dilke repeats the nonsense, just as Mr. Fawcett gives it currency as Postmaster General, because communicated on what is presumed to be "good authority." But Sir Charles Dilke and Mr. Fawcett alike know that "good authority" never was wanting, and never will be wanting, to sustain a lucrative superstition; and when they consider that the authorities which answer for Vaccination profit by Vaccination, and by Vaccination design to profit yet more, they should think twice, yea thrice, before they consent to lend their names to float statements which, from their origin, ought to excite suspicion and inquiry.

VIII.—THE INVACCINATION OF SYPHILIS.

"Then as to the alleged Invaccination of Syphilis, we "have the evidence of Mr. Jonathan Hutchinson to the "effect that Syphilis cannot be conveyed by pure lymph "even from a syphilitic child."

When Mr. Hutchinson was before the Vaccination Committee in 1871, he was inclined to the opinion that when Syphilis was invaccinated it was with virus mixed with blood, it having been "proved that blood can transfer Syphilis." Pressed as to whether virus, or so-called "lymph," being produced from blood, might not also convey the disease, he answered very properly—

"*It is not a subject on which I should like to infer anything; I should like to have experiments and facts.*" No. 5073.

Thus it would have been untrue to say in 1871, that Mr. Hutchinson gave evidence to "the effect that Syphilis cannot be conveyed by pure lymph even from a syphilitic child." On the contrary, he expressly guarded himself from such an inference, saying, "I should like to have experiments and facts."

Twelve years have elapsed since 1871, and much has been learnt in the interval. Mr. Hutchinson has not been idle, and in his *Illustrations of Clinical Surgery*, Fasc. vi., p. 130, 1877, he writes—

"Next, we may ask, is it absolutely necessary that blood should be used in Vaccination in order to convey Syphilis? *It seems highly probable that it is not.* At anyrate there is not the least evidence in three of the series of cases which I have recorded that the lymph used was visibly contaminated with blood."

The invaccination of Syphilis, with blood or without blood, is now beyond dispute. It is the ghastly risk of Vaccination according to Sir Thomas Watson, the dread of which he held sufficient to justify firm resistance to its infliction. The general resort to Animal Vaccination on the Continent and America, and the offer of the alternative by our own authorities, attest the reality and frequency of the danger. It is as idle to argue against such practical evidence as to enforce it. The convenient practice of arm-to-arm Vaccination has not been abandoned for the difficult and uncertain calf-to-calf practice without grave and sufficient reason.

In making the untruthful assertion as to the evidence of Mr. Hutchinson, it is not to be supposed that Sir Charles Dilke spoke of himself. He had probably never bestowed a thought on the subject until he received his instructions from the medical officials of the Board he represents—officials who know the facts as well as we do. Misled himself, Sir Charles was put up to fulfil the prescription of Mr. May, and "preserve Vaccination from reproach." We have in the procedure an instructive illustration of what Mrs. Leslie Stephen too confidingly describes as "lying freely," the House of Commons and the public being treated as invalids for whom truth might be dangerous; whilst Anti-Vaccinists, as enemies of the human race, fall under the more unscrupulous dispensation of Lord Wolseley.

IX.—As Concerns Switzerland.

"The Hon. Member for Leicester claims that the ex-
"perience of Germany is on his side, and spoke generally
"as if there were a growth of European opinion in that
"direction. I cannot admit that my Hon. Friend is
"correct. I believe that in one Swiss canton the
"compulsory law has been repealed, but since 1871
"Denmark, Holland, Roumania, Spain, and Germany
"have made changes in the direction of Compulsory
"Vaccination."

Naturally we should prefer the evidence of Mr. P. A.
Taylor to that of Sir Charles Dilke as to the movement
of European opinion in the matter of Vaccination, inasmuch as Mr. Taylor has made it his business to know
where Sir Charles has no motive for knowledge. Such
would be our prepossession; and when we descend to
detail we find it justified. Sir Charles is pleased to
"believe that in one Swiss canton the compulsory law
has been repealed": when we compare this belief with
the facts, and remember that Sir Charles was brought
from the Foreign Office to preside over the Local
Government Board, we discover how possible it is to be
in the way of information and remain ignorant—
especially when information is undesirable.

In 1882 Switzerland was profoundly agitated. Under
medical dictation a law on epidemics had been passed
by the Federal Council in which Vaccination was the
leading article, enforced with penalties of extraordinary
severity. Much satisfaction was expressed in this country over the thorough-going legislation, and we were
called upon to recognise the wisdom of the Swiss, and
their superiority to our ridiculous scruples, physiological
and political, in connection with Vaccination. But the

satisfaction was premature. The Swiss people had to be reckoned with. The law was promulgated, but the people did not like it, and it was resolved to submit the medical legislation to the popular vote. This right of appeal to the national judgment can only be exercised within 90 days, and must be claimed with at least 30,000 signatures. 80,000 were, however, affixed to the demand, and on the 30th of July the decision of the nation was taken with the following results—

The Twenty-five Cantons of the Swiss Confederation.	July 30, 1882.			Per Cent.	
The Cantons are set in order, according to their negative votes. Neuenburg or Neuchâtel alone accepted the Act.	Number of citizens entitled to vote.	Voted.	Rejected the Act.	From 100 entitled Voted.	Of 100 votes Negative.
Uri,...........................	4,160	2,715	2,656	65	98
Appenzell, Interior,........	3,265	2,080	2,028	64	98
Glarus,........................	8,178	5,215	4,923	64	94
Wallis, ...	26,083	14,604	13,730	56	94
Appenzell, Exterior,.......	12,221	10,460	9,745	86	93
Nidwalden, ...	2,835	1,061	969	37	91
Schwyz,......................	12,380	3,042	2,769	25	91
Freiburg, ...	27,824	15,542	14,078	56	91
St. Gallen, ...	50,826	36,642	33,172	72	91
Baselstadt, ...	10,008	4,742	4,153	47	88
Obwalden, ...	3,726	1,124	979	30	87
Luzern, ...	31,332	12,365	10,536	39	85
Bern,.........................	109,256	42,661	36,172	39	85
Baselland, ...	11,272	5,655	4,566	50	81
Aargau,......................	42,041	31,891	25,417	76	80
Zug,..........................	5,688	1,787	1,412	31	79
Tessin, ...	35,000	10,157	7,450	29	73
Solothurn, ...	16,708	6,247	4,566	37	73
Thurgau, ...	23,866	16,568	12,034	69	73
Graubünden, ...	22,426	12,905	9,241	58	72
Waadt,.......................	58,326	14,829	9,734	25	66
Schaffhausen, ...	8,021	6,247	4,093	78	66
Genf,.........................	20,034	4,377	2,673	22	61
Zürich,.......................	73,904	52,725	34,672	71	61
Neuenburg, ...	23,174	6,147	2,200	27	36
All Switzerland,............	642,554	321,788	253,968	50	79

The results of the vote have been tabulated for us by Professor A. Vogt, of Berne University, himself a leader of his countrymen in repelling the mercenary aggression on their liberties and intelligence.

Of this significant and conclusive demonstration against compulsory Vaccination, Sir Charles Dilke either knew nothing, or affected to know nothing. He believed the compulsory law had been repealed in one Swiss canton !

When the nullification of the vicious legislation was reported in this country, we were officiously reminded that enactments in favour of Vaccination remained in force in the majority of the cantons, which was true ; but, as we observed, the fair expectation was that the national rejection of compulsory Vaccination would presently lead to the repeal of the said cantonal enactments. So it has proved, and more rapidly than we dared to hope. Compulsory Vaccination has been abolished in the Federal Army and in the cantons of Basel, Glarus, Luzern, Zürich, and Schaffhausen, and suspended under the influence of public opinion in Bern, St. Gallen, Aargau and Graubünden. In Uri and Geneva compulsion has never been exercised.

There is, therefore, good hope that Vaccination throughout Switzerland will become more and more discredited, and drop into disuse, the process being hastened by the marked improvement in public health, and especially the health of the young.

Sir Charles Dilke referred to Holland, but Holland is not likely to lag far behind Switzerland. Compulsion has just been withdrawn from Vaccination in the Netherlands Army in consequence of unquestionable disasters ;

and opinion is so balanced in the Chambers that at any time we may hear the people are set free like the soldiers. As for the other countries named by Sir Charles Dilke, it is unnecessary to enter into doubtful controversy. When Vaccination begins to go, it will go rapidly. We often hear of its acceptance by peoples savage and superstitious, and of the wonders it achieves among them ; but so much we take as of course. Vaccination is a rite that suits the savage and superstitious, and the disposition of the civilised toward it is doubtless due to the survival of similar instincts. It harmonises with confidence in charms and incantations—means by which laziness hopes to get much out of little, and to constrain the favour of unseen powers by artifices which brutes might disdain.

X.—THE LAW OF REPEATED PENALTIES.

"The Hon. Member for Stockport says the most " sacred point with the Local Government Board is the " enforcement of Vaccination under repeated penalty. " Before the Committee of 1871 a Scottish witness gave " evidence that there were no cases of repeated penalties " in Scotland, but that still there was much more com- " plete immunity from Smallpox and more general Vac- " cination than in England. That Committee, in their " report, expressed doubt as to the wisdom of the law of " repeated penalties. The Local Government Board are " of opinion that repeated penalties defeat their own " object and do not secure the proper observance of the " law, and the proper respect for the law, but the Board " are doubtful whether that is the view of the House of " Commons."

The Vaccination Committee in 1871 did not "express doubt as to the wisdom of the law of repeated penalties"; they went further; they recommended—

"That whenever in any case two penalties, or one full penalty, have been imposed upon a parent, the magistrate should not impose any further penalty in respect of the same child."

This recommendation, embodied in a new Vaccination Act, was the subject of a short debate in the House of Commons on 15th August, 1871, and was carried on division by 57 to 12; but in the House of Lords on 18th August, its rejection was moved by Lord Redesdale, and when their Lordships divided, the Contents were 7, the Non-Contents 8—majority, 1! On 19th August the House of Commons considered the Lords' amendment, when Mr. W. E. Forster observed—

"The House of Lords has struck out of the Bill the 10th Clause—the important clause which mitigates penalties. The clause was passed in this House by a majority of 57 to 12, and expunged in the other House by a majority of 8 to 7; the total number of peers voting being just equal to the number of members of the Select Committee which, after long and careful consideration, came to a unanimous conclusion in favour of the clause! I should have no hesitation in asking the House to disagree to the amendment if the period of the session would allow of such disagreement being made without loss of the Bill; but as that is not the case, and as such a course may involve the loss of the Bill, which effects several great improvements, I fear the House has no choice, and must accept the amendment. I regret the omission of the clause, because in my opinion it strikes a heavy blow at the principle of Compulsory Vaccination, which their lordships, as well as I, think necessary for the health of the country."

Mr. M'Laren said—

"Whilst I concur in the course proposed, I hope the Government may lose no time in bringing in a Bill to enact the clause that is dropped."

The motion was agreed to, and the Lords' nullification of the clause accepted. Nothing more was done, and repeated penalties continue to be enforced with irregular injustice.

Repeated penalties, we may add, originated under

Section 31 of the Vaccination Act of 1867, which made the existence of an unvaccinated child a continuous offence on the part of the parent or guardian, up to the age of fourteen. At the time, Mr. Thomas Chambers prophesied in the House of Commons—

"I am persuaded that when the Bill is passed an agitation will commence which will never cease until the Act is repealed."

The prediction of Sir Thomas Chambers proceeds to fulfilment. Whilst we condemn the hardship and tyranny of the bad law erratically administered, we have yet to admit that more than aught else it has been the means of advertising Vaccination, compelling inquiry into the origin and varieties of the imposture, creating sympathy with sufferers under its infliction, giving courage to resistance, and begetting agitation and organisation for the overthrow of the infamous law. Unquestionably the Local Government Board is right— "these repeated penalties have defeated their own object"; and, in Mr. Forster's words, "have struck a heavy blow at the principle of Compulsory Vaccination." When we consider the misery and outrage to which poor and faithful parents have been subjected under repeated penalties, it is impossible to rejoice without reserve that through them we shall achieve deliverance from a cruel and mischievous delusion. Nevertheless, we may recall Bishop Thirlwall's observation—"Whilst I should hesitate to say that whatever is, is best, I have a strong faith that it is *for* the best, and that the general stream of tendency is toward good."

XI.—SIR JOSEPH PEASE IN REQUISITION.

"I should have thought a more practical debate than
" the debate on the question whether Vaccination is
" good or bad might have been raised, if my Hon.
" Friend, the Member for South Durham (Sir Joseph W.
" Pease), brought before the House a motion which
" would directly test the opinion of the House on the
" question of repeated penalties. It is because I am
" favourable to Vaccination that I desire to see a change
" in the law in this respect. If the view of the Hon.
" Member for South Durham is against repeated penal-
" ties, he had better raise that question directly before
" the House, and bring forward a motion on the subject.
" I do not think it is a case for inquiry by a Select
" Committee. The object would not be served by an
" inquiry, for we have already the unanimous report of a
" Committee of the House adverse to repeated penalties."

Here be strategy! The officials of the Local Government Board are against repeated penalties. Sir Charles
Dilke is against repeated penalties. A Select Committee of the House of Commons condemned repeated
penalties. The Government introduced a bill in 1880
to abolish repeated penalties. Yet here is Sir Charles
Dilke urging Sir Joseph Pease "to raise the question
directly before the House"! Why, why should Sir
Joseph Pease be invited to force an open door?

The reason is not recondite. The Government in
1880, in the first flush of vigour and virtue determined
to modify a great wrong. It was known that over large
parts of the country repeated penalties were not exacted;
and where exacted, were chiefly from men humble and
faithful, who, abhorring Vaccination, incurred the wrath
of parochial dignitaries, who made use of the law to

avenge their flouted authority, not unfrequently mounting the bench as magistrates to consummate the persecution they had initiated as guardians. Such scandals, manifold and notorious, not only brought Vaccination into disrepute, but put justice to shame in letting out law to satiate personal malice. To abate such iniquity the Evesham Letter was written, and liberally administered, but its intention was not clearly apparent, and was often ineffective. Its terms are well known : Prosecute recusants energetically, but when you ascertain they will not submit, then cease prosecuting, lest their successful resistance beget sympathy, and per· chance imitation, to the further discredit of the law. A wonderful man was Shakspere ; this Evesham Letter he foreshadowed with an accuracy almost startling. Thus—

DOGBERRY.—This is your charge : You shall comprehend all vagrom men ; you are to bid any man stand in the prince's name.

2ND WATCH.—How if he will not stand ?

DOGBERRY.—Why then, take no note of him, but let him go ; and presently call the watch together, and thank God you are rid of a knave.

Here we have the Letter in précis, in itself a dull and involved affair ; and some perplexity would be spared if the Shaksperian version were adopted as preamble. Politicians often live to sigh with Ophelia, " Lord, we know what we are, but know not what we may be." To think that Sir Charles Dilke, the pink and flower of young Radicalism, should be called to play Dogberry, and be pleased to play Dogberry, holding it to be the only practicable part under the circumstances !

The motive of the Government therefore in proposing to do away with repeated penalties, erratically exacted was clear and capable of complete justification in the

interest of Vaccination ; but a lion appeared in the way.
The craft arose insurgent. Medical deputations, artfully
multiplied, swarmed around Mr. Dodson. Poor Mr.
Spottiswoode, President of the Royal Society, was
dragged up to testify that if repeated penalties were
surrendered, science itself would be in danger. Worst
of all, the name of Gladstone had got associated with
Blasphemy, and if to Blasphemy the Opposition could
adjoin Smallpox, it was considered nothing could save
the Administration. Wherefore it was decided to drop
the Bill, and go on mitigating injustice with the Evesham Letter.

We said there was a lion in the way, but we meant a
more formidable animal, an ass, the British Ass, which
Carlyle use to say was too much overlooked—

> The British Lion has his fame,
>   And shall it come to pass,
> That none will urge another claim,
>   And praise the British Ass?
> How long his ears, how loud his bray,
>   Profoundly stupid he,
> And ever toward the proper way,
>   His *tail* points faithfully.

It was the dread of the Ass which prevailed, and in the
words of Mr. Bright, at the time a member of the Government, it was with extreme regret that a measure so
eminently just was withdrawn. Such being the situation,
we can understand Sir Charles Dilke's suggestion, that
Sir Joseph Pease should lend his paw to whisk that
particular chestnut out of the fire.

We have in the circumstances an instructive illustration of the new order of statesmanship in which men in
power do not presume to enforce what they think just,
but consider what can be advocated in the House of

Commons without endangering their majority. In the matter of repeated penalties for non-vaccination, we do not doubt that a clear and candid explanation of the state of the law, and its irregular and arbitrary administration, would have carried the Government bill through Parliament; but the fear of the British Ass—of being charged with the diffusion of Smallpox was too much for nerves shaken with the bray about Blasphemy.

Whilst we should gladly see repeated penalties abolished, we have little to say for a measure so inadequate. The law as it exists has wrought for us exceedingly. It has made us Ironsides. There are no more enthusiastic and indomitable Anti-Vaccinists than those who have undergone the ordeal of repeated prosecutions. The law has done its work, and whether it is modified is now of little consequence. A force has been evoked that will only be brought to rest when Vaccination is overthrown.

A FAIR PROPOSAL.

AFTER the debate and division of the 19th June, I had
an interview with an M.P. who did not vote.   He said
he was favourable to some modification of the compulsory law, but held that the motion of Mr. Taylor and
Mr. Hopwood went too far, and had no chance of acceptance by the House of Commons.   It would have been
far more sensible had they taken up the measure introduced by the Government in 1880, which he should
have gladly supported.

I replied that Mr. Taylor and Mr. Hopwood were
experienced politicians who knew what they were about.
It was not their business to establish the law of Compulsory Vaccination by making it less odious.   *That*
the Gladstone Ministry undertook to do, and were terrified out of by the medical trade unions.   The difficulty
of repeated penalties was not Mr. Taylor's affair, but
that of the Administration, as Sir Charles Dilke confessed, and as Mr. Sclater-Booth allowed.   The injustice
of repeated penalties, their abrogation in many parishes,
and their remorseless infliction in others, the defiance
they excite, and the open and ignominious defeat they
impose upon the law, were scandals which advertise the
absurdities of Vaccination, and extend the area of resistance, thereby promoting Mr. Taylor's radical purposes.
It was simply cowardice on the part of the Governmeut
which deferred amendment of the law ; but, I repeated,
such an amendment in the interest of Vaccination was
not Mr. Taylor's business.   Indeed, with what grace
could he advocate a measure in his opinion altogether

inadequate, and which he must advise his followers to disown as any proper satisfaction of their righteous demands.

The reasonableness of this contention was admitted, but it was urged that as practical men we were bound to formulate some proposition which Parliament could accept, and yet which we could reconcile to our consciences as helping us on our way. Why, for instance, should we hesitate to submit to a fixed fine as a proof of sincerity and a license for indulgence?

That, I replied, was, in other words the proposal of the Government in 1880—"that no parent should be liable to be convicted of negligence who had either paid the full penalty of 20s., or had been twice adjudged to pay any penalty in respect of a child." 20s. was to be the price of freedom from the infliction of "an acute specific disease," according to the definition of Vaccinators—or from blood-poisoning at hazard as we regard the rite.

Viewed as a business transaction we object to the proposition. We are in the enjoyment of better terms already. In numerous parishes repeated prosecutions for refusal to vaccinate are rarely attempted, whilst penalties range at a lower figure than 20s. In some parishes where it is known that parents seriously object to Vaccination, they are let alone on the tacit understanding that they keep quiet about their exemption. And in certain other parishes where guardians are opposed to Vaccination, the rite is surrendered to private discretion. The proposal, therefore, of a fixed fine has nothing to recommend it beyond the exchange of covenanted for uncovenanted mercy, and the withdrawal of the law from vindictive application by fanatics who do not happen to be amenable to the Evesham Letter.

But, I continued, the suggestion of any fine is insufferable, and that it should be entertained illustrates the plutocratic imbecility of our legislators. As it is, many Anti-Vaccinists escape prosecution because of their wealth. It would show bad taste to affront them, and any possible penalties could be so much wanton annoyance. But to men in humble circumstances, the penalties — which to the wealthy are not worth a thought, are serious indeed, representing hardship and privation without limit; and it is against such humble folk, who presume to have an opinion in opposition to their " betters," that parsons and other parochial tyrants delight to harass with the extreme malignity of the law. The time draws near when legislation which thus discriminates the rich from the poor, turning to the poor the sharper edge of the law, will be an infamy impossible.

Still, I felt there was something reasonable in the demand of my M.P., that we should frame a proposition which might be submitted to a Parliament of Vaccinists with some chance of acceptance—which, although it might fall far short of our complete intention, should not be inconsistent with it.

Thereon I reminded him of Mr. Danby P. Fry's suggestion before the Vaccination Committee of 1871—

" To meet the case of conscientious objections, it might " perhaps, be worthy of consideration whether a parent " might not be exempted from the penalty who takes " an oath, or makes an affirmation, that he has a con- " scientious objection to the vaccination of his child." No. 3845.

Whatever may be our opinion of Vaccination in itself, or of the wisdom of the State in promoting and supporting its practice, such a provision would not only provide relief for the oppressed, but means for a trustworthy test of the comparative resistance of the Vaccinated and Unvaccinated to Smallpox. Impressed with this conviction, I had written to Mr. Gladstone as follows—

TO THE RIGHT HON. WILLIAM E. GLADSTONE, M.P.

London, 1st October, 1880.

Sir,—Knowing the pressure of your numerous and grave duties, I yet venture to draw your attention to a great wrong that you may exercise your power for its cessation.

Some days ago Robert Tweedale, of Rochdale, was taken from his bed at night, close by the residence of your colleague, Mr. Bright, and conveyed to the County Prison, where he was treated as a convict. Why? Because, as a wise and tender parent, he refused to have his child vaccinated. The law under which this outrage was committed is, in the words of Mr. Bright, "Monstrous, and ought to be repealed." Yet is it not repealed.

Cases like that of Tweedale's are of frequent occurrence, and I and others who are persuaded that Vaccination is a useless and hurtful superstition, find it difficult to express in terms that do not savour of violence the indignation aroused by such deeds of brutal oppression.

I put it to your reason and conscience, why should such outrages be permitted on my reason and conscience? Are only Theological convictions entitled to liberty and respect? Are those who entertain unpopular opinions,

11

scientific or social, to be abandoned without pity to the wild beasts of bigotry? The rite of Vaccination is said to secure its subjects from Smallpox. Let those who trust in the rite be satisfied with their own security. Being secure, why should they inflict it on the unwilling and unbelieving? If we have Smallpox, they cannot take it. If they say they can, they surrender the pretext under which the rite is enforced.

Your Government introduced a Bill last session to abolish repeated penalties for non-Vaccination, but whether from lack of opportunity or inclination, it was not pressed upon the House of Commons. The Bill, however, excited much alarm in the medical trade-unions; and it was said that in allowing dissenters from Vaccination to escape with limited punishment, you were preparing to sell indulgences to law-breakers, whilst contriving to oppress the poor with fines and costs that were to them overwhelming; and there was truth in the criticism.

Summarily, I would observe that no relaxation of the Vaccination Acts will ever be assented to by the medical corporations. You have shared in the abolition of many abuses, but did you ever abolish one with the good-will of those whose advantage, real or imaginary, consisted in the abuse? Wherefore, I say, if you have not the courage to confront the medical profession in this matter, I shall plead with you, for the present, in vain. But if you are resolved to make good the hope of relief held out to us, I pray you simplify, justify, and dignify your measure by the entire removal of money penalties. Let Vaccination Officers be authorised to receive objections to Vaccination on affidavit before a Justice of the Peace.

Let children thus exempted be carefully registered as Unvaccinated, and await the verdict of experience.

At present the Unvaccinated afford no data for a just comparison with the Vaccinated. The Unvaccinated are those who are rejected as too feeble to undergo the Vaccine Fever, or those who are the offspring of the wretched and the homeless, and thus escape detection by Vaccination Officers. With whatever disease afflicted, the Unvaccinated would therefore compare unfavourably with the Vaccinated. The children of disbelievers in Vaccination would, on the other hand, afford a fair test of the advantage of unpolluted blood. The experiment would not only be valuable in a scientific sense, but it would be a worthy exploit on the part of statesmen, whose profession is hatred of oppression and reverence for the rights of man.—Yours faithfully,

WILLIAM WHITE.

Whilst making a proposal like the foregoing, I lay little stress upon it. Statesmen, so far as I have observed, care little for justice except in so far as it can be converted into personal capital. The oppressed, until they can make themselves feared, or can be turned to practical account, are treated with indifference. In politics as in war, those who would have must take. It is not for us to wait upon politicians, but to make ourselves formidable to them; to give them no rest until they consent to go with us. We shall use every means to expose and discredit Vaccination. We shall thwart the compulsory law by every device in our power. We shall organise resistance. We shall encourage the timid, and support the

poor in resistance, and shall take care that none suffer
secretly or for naught.   And throughout we shall prefer
practice to preaching; for in this movement we have
realised anew the ancient discovery, that the blood of
the martyrs is the seed of the Church.

***

SOMETHING MORE ABOUT THE FRANCO-GERMAN WAR STATISTICS.

[From *The Vaccination Inquirer*, November, 1883.]

THE mystification, sufficiently exposed, of the 23,469
French and 263 German soldiers who died of Smallpox
in the course of the Franco-German War of 1870-71,
appears to have been recited with a curious variation in
the great Council of Berne, on the 6th February of the
current year.   In a debate on Compulsory Vaccination,
Herr Steiger, Minister of the Interior, begged to draw
special attention to the colossal difference between the
Smallpox fatalities in the respective armies.   "From June,
1870, to July, 1871," he said, "the Germans lost 3,162
men from Smallpox; whilst the French lost 23,469 in
the same time and in the same districts;" adding, "this
statistic cannot be too often repeated."   Poor Steiger!
he little knew that the French 23,469 was entirely myth-
ical; nor could he foresee that Sir Lyon Playfair would
in the English House of Commons, on 19th June, reduce
the German 3,162 to the paltry figure of 261 or 263, on
what he described as "the best authority"!   Colossal,
indeed, was the difference, and, strange to say, according
to Herr Steiger, it was confined to Smallpox; for "actually the French lost fewer men from Typhus than did

the Germans." Very mysterious it is, as it ever is mysterious when fancy gets among statistics. The French own they do not know how many men perished of Smallpox in the war, and, so far as we can ascertain, the Germans are no more accurately informed. In the havoc and confusion of a contest like that of 1870-71, there was much to excuse imperfect and lost reckoning. Anyhow, it is for us to disregard statistics evolved from the inner consciousness of unknown persons intent on promoting the cause of Vaccination.

To complete the curious story, we should remind our readers that Dr. Thilenius, speaking before the Petitions Committee of the Reichstag, on 29th January, said—

"The arguments of the Anti-Vaccinators are absolutely irreconcileable with the exceedingly small number of Smallpox deaths in the properly vaccinated German Army, when compared with the perfectly colossal Smallpox mortality in the French Army. According to Roth, the full number of Smallpox deaths in the German Army, in the war of 1870-71, was only 261, against nearly 24,000 in the inefficiently vaccinated French Army. Those who are not convinced by such proofs of the protective power of Vaccination, will not be convinced by anything. But all these overpowering facts have as yet produced no impression on the Anti-Vaccinators, and they will continue as heretofore to gainsay them."

The hard-headed Anti-Vaccinators! Nothing would persuade them to believe in the death of 24,000 French soldiers ; and their disbelief is now justified. Turning it the other way, how such figures were credited by anybody is the marvel, representing, as they must have done, at least 150,000 cases—an immense army paralysed with Smallpox, a miraculous phenomenon unheard of until the war was over! But, accepting the figures, in what respect did they prove, as Dr. Thilenius held, "the protective power of Vaccination"? The French soldiers were all revaccinated, and yet 24,000 of them

died of Smallpox! Could there possibly be a more overwhelming demonstration of the inutility of Vaccination?
It has been said "the age of myths is past," but that is
a mistake. Certain forms of myth may have become
impossible, but myth formation is active as ever; and in
an atmosphere of suitable faith nothing is incredible.
Here we have an absolute creation of fancy, in its very
terms improbable, yet vouched for within the present
year before three Legislatures—in Germany by Dr.
Thilenius, in Switzerland by Herr Steiger, and in England by Sir Lyon Playfair, and taken everywhere for
gospel; and save for the exposure effected by Anti-
Vaccinators, the fiction might have passed on as veritable
history! Even now we do not flatter ourselves that we
have seen the last of it. As has been observed, "A convenient lie has a sort of immortality."

[Also from *The Vaccination Inquirer*, December, 1883.]

Again we revert to the statistic of Smallpox in the
Franco-German War. The 23,469 Frenchmen who
perished are disowned by the French War-Office, and
surrendered by Dr. W. B. Carpenter; but what of the 263
Germans who were played against the 23,469 Frenchmen? Last month we expressed a doubt as to whether
the German authorities were much more accurately informed than the French as to their losses from Smallpox in the great struggle; and our doubt is verified.
Mr. G. S. Gibbs had addressed an inquiry on the subject
to Berlin, and was thus answered—

"ARMY MEDICAL DEPARTMENT,
WAR OFFICE.

"No. 691/7.   M. M. A.

"BERLIN, 30th July, 1883.

"In reply to your letter of July 6, to his Excellency the Minister of War,
the Chief Clerk forwards a certified extract from the Register of those who

died of Smallpox in the *Prussian* army in the several months of the years 1869, 1870, and 1871." [This shows 1 death in 1869, in the month of August; none in 1870; in 1871, 3 deaths in July, 6 in August, 6 in September, 10 in November, and 12 in December.] "*For the time* from July, 1870, to June, 1871 (the twelve months of the war), the numbers wished for are not recorded, and regret is expressed that on this account the desired information cannot be given. TOLER LISOUKE.

"To George S. Gibbs, Esq.,
"Derry Lodge, Darlington."

Thus do the 263 Germans follow the 23,469 Frenchmen into the realm of fiction! The marvellous statistic with which Sir Lyon Playfair astonished the House of Commons, and drew an ecstatic compliment from Sir Charles Dilke, is at last recognised for fabulous beyond dispute. What shall be said of a cause thus defended? What shall we think of an advocate who picks up figures he knows not where, and vouches for them as authentic because they happen to lie for Vaccination?

INDEX.

Ague the curse of life, 137.

Algiers, soldiers invaccinated with Syphilis, 14, 131.

Alison, Sir Archibald, 138.

America, Vaccination in, 96.

Antimony, Tartarated, Pref. xvi.

Anti-Vaccinator, 67.

Army, British, Smallpox in, 75-76.

Arnold, Arthur, 3.

Ballard, Dr., Vaccination a real disease, 10; invaccinated Syphilis. 11; Smallpox not to be exterminated, 43, 97; the 1871 epidemic, 61.

Barran, John, 3.

Bayard, Dr., Revaccination of French Army, 64.

Berlin, 1871-72 epidemic, 71; in 1746 and 1871, 73; war office, 167.

Bickersteth, 128.

Birkenhead epidemic, 86, 94.

Bismarck, 70.

Black Death 64, 71.

Blane, Sir Gilbert, 27.

Blennerhassett, R. P., 3.

Boston, 1752 epidemic, 89; Smallpox, 90, 96.

Brick, Jefferson, 97.

Bright, Jacob, 4.

Bright, John, regrets Dodson's bill, 123; the law is monstrous, 161.

British Medical Journal, 49, 67, 122.

Bronchitis, 15, 18, 19.

Buchanan, Dr., his 12,000 London infants, 3; memorandum on London Smallpox, 83, 84, 85.

Burt, Thomas, 4.

Busch's *Bismarck*, 70.

Cameron, Dr. C., cause of increased Smallpox, 60.

Carpenter. Dr. Alfred, extinction of Smallpox by cleanliness, 42, 57; would arrest children for Vaccination, 116; increase of virulence in transfer by virus, 134.

Carpenter, Dr. W. B., 17, 67; an incontinent pledge, 68; *Vaccination Inquirer*, 90; Queens Mary and Victoria, 109; answered by P. A. Taylor, 125; his miraculous statistic, 166.

Carter, R. Brudenell, invaccinated Syphilis, 11.

Catechism, Dr. Garth Wilkinson's, 59.

Cattle Plague Commission, 47.

Ceely, Robert, Pref. xiv.

Chadwick, Edwin, "keep your eye on the death-rate," 139.

Chambers, Sir Thomas, 4, 103.

Chambers, Sir William, 54.

Christ's Hospital, 88.

Cobbett to Wilberforce, 8.

Cohen, Arthur, 4.

Colin, Dr. Leon, Smallpox in Franco-German war, 66; treatment of Smallpox, 70.

Collins, Dr. W. J., Vaccine Erysipelas, 17; reply to Playfair, Pref. viii.

Conference on Animal Vaccination, 61.

Consumption, 15, 18.

Corn Laws, 5.

Corrigan, Sir D., 46.

Cory, Dr., syphilised himself, 13.

Cowen, Joseph, 4.

Cowpox, Jenner on, 97.

Cowpox and Smallpox Cowpox, Pref. xiii.

Cowpox Factory, Pref. xiv.

Craig, Wm. V., 4.

Cromwell, 6.

Cross on Norwich epidemic, 86.

HAY NISBET & Co., PRINTERS, 38 STOCKWELL STREET, GLASGOW.

www.ingramcontent.com/pod-product-compliance
Lightning Source LLC
Chambersburg PA
CBHW030842270326
41928CB00007B/1180